Bonaire History and Culture for tourism

Bonaire environment

Author

Clyde Hill

Copyright Notice

First Printing: 2017.

ISBN: 978-1-912483-38-9

Publisher: Global Print Digital.
Arlington Row, Bibury, Cirencester GL7 5ND
Gloucester
United Kingdom.
Website: www.homeworkoffer.com

.

Table of Content

Introduction 1

History 3

Culture 14

    Bonaire's Culture 14

    Simadan Festival 18

    Celebrations 20

    Tradition 21

    Music & Instruments 21

    Local Artists 22

    Traditional Dress 22

    Papiamentu 23

Economy 28

Tourism 30

    Bon Bini 30

    Travel Guide 32

    Travel Tips 34

    Weather 36

    Visas and Vaccinations 38

    Transportation 40

    Food and Restaurants 41

        Dining & Restaurants 45

    Airports 70

    Attractions 72

    Shopping and Leisure 76

    Festivals and Events 78

    Things to Do 81

        Museum 83

        Night Life 84

        Rock Climbing 85

        Sailing & Boating 87

        Snorkeling Tips 87

        Diving and Snorkeling 93

        Bonaire Marine Park 93

            History: 94

        Scuba Diving 101

        BonaireBird Watching 104

        Flora & Fauna 105

            Flamingos 107

Birds 109

Stinapa 114

Karko Project 115

Coral Restoration Project 116

Sea Turtle Conservation Bonaire 117

Echo Bonaire 118

Beaches 120

Getting Around 122

Car Rentals 122

Motorcycle, Scooter and Bicycle Rentals 123

Transportation & Taxi 124

Cycling 124

Introduction

About our Culture- A History

The Bonairean culture is reflected in the faces of her people. Its origins are as varied as are the ethnic roots of the 19,000 plus residents. The real Bonairean culture is based on traditions that go back many generations and are chronicled in the songs and dances that are performed during holidays and festivals. It is also based on strong family ties and a general respect for nature and an understanding of an environment that originally was foreign to those first settlers and slaves that were forced to work the inhospitable, arid land.

Those early days of slavery conditioned the people to be strong in the face of adversity. And, it was during this time that the spirit of the people began to develop and they made up songs, invented dances, and began to sing in the old African Tradition. These songs and dances evolved into festivals and have survived to become an important part of life and culture on Bonaire.

History

Although Bonaire's future seems inextricably entwined with its remarkable coastal reefs and its austere natural beauty, the island's past is tied to an altogether different set of resources and attributes. With a comfortably dry climate and steady trade winds (the very conditions that have made it a windsurfing mecca), Bonaire has long been recognized as an ideal locale for the production of salt. For over three centuries, the island's culture and prosperity was dependent upon this most important of the world's spices. Salt is still produced on Bonaire, though the stunning salt beds of Pekelmeer are also home to one of the hemisphere's great populations of flamingoes.

To bring a rich history into context, meet Adelfa St. Jago, Honorable Leader of Culture, explaining the importance of history in the video below by Jermaine Fletcher.

Bonaire's first inhabitants were the Caiquetios, a branch of the Arawak Indians who sailed across from what is now Venezuela around 1000 AD. Traces of Caiquetio culture are visible at a number of archaeological sites, including those at Lac Bay and northeast of Kralendijk. Bonaire HistoryRock paintings and petroglyphs have survived at the caves at Spelonk, Onima, Ceru Pungi, and Ceru Crita-Cabai. The Caiquetios were apparently a very tall people, for the Spanish dubbed the Leeward Islands 'las Islas de los Gigantes' (the islands of the giants). The name the Caiquetios gave to their island was adapted into Spanish as 'Boynay.'

After a falling out with Queen Isabella in 1495, Columbus lost his exclusive rights to explore the New World, and the Caribbean became open territory. Alonso de Ojeda and Amerigo Vespucci (from whom the Americas derive their name) were among the first to take advantage of the situation: in 1499 they landed on Bonaire and claimed it for Spain. Bonaire had neither gold nor sufficient rainfall to encourage large-scale agricultural production, so the Spanish saw very little reason to develop the colony. Instead, they forced the native Caiquetios into slavery on the large plantations of the island of Hispaniola. By 1515, Bonaire had been mostly depopulated.

Bonaire HistoryIn 1526, Juan de Ampues, governor of Bonaire, Curacao, and Aruba, began to raise cattle on the island. He brought in a number of Caiquetios and some Indians from Venezuela as laborers, and within a few years cows, sheep, goats, pigs, donkeys, and horses were being raised on the island. Valued less for their meat than for their hides, the animals needed little tending and were generally let loose to wander freely around the island. Before long they greatly outnumbered the human inhabitants, and today the island counts substantial populations of donkeys and goats among its wildlife.

Over the next few centuries, few of the island's inhabitants were to arrive willingly. There was a small inland settlement at Rincon, safe from the predations of pirates, but development was not encouraged as it was in other, richer colonies. Bonaire's immigrants were mostly convicts from the Spanish colonies in South America. Dutch admiral Boudewijn Hendricksz dropped off a group of Spanish and Portuguese prisoners, who founded the town of Antriol. For much of the next 300 years, even after the island was ceded to the Dutch, Bonaire remained a notorious penal colony.

Bonaire Slave HutsIn 1633, the Dutch, having lost the island of St. Maarten to the Spanish, retaliated by capturing Curacao, Bonaire, and Aruba. While Curacao emerged as a center of the slave trade, Bonaire became a plantation of the Dutch West India Company. A small number of African slaves were put to work cultivating dyewood and maize and harvesting solar salt around Blue Pan. They were joined by the few remaining Indians and convicts. Slave quarters, rising no higher than a man's waist and built entirely of stone, still stand in the area around Rincon and along the saltpans as a grim reminder of Bonaire's repressive past.

From the beginning of the seventeenth century until the middle of the nineteenth, only the military personnel who supervised the plantations and the prison houses were allowed on the island. When the Dutch West India Company dissolved in 1791, its properties were confiscated by the Dutch government, which continued operations on Bonaire. The slaves, now owned by the Kingdom of the Netherlands, came to be known as 'government slaves,' or, in Papiamentu , 'Katibu di Rei,' meaning 'slaves of the king.' Although the slaves were allowed to grow and sell their own produce, and sometimes even to buy their own freedom, living conditions on Bonaire worsened. By 1835, rumors of an uprising began to circulate around an escaped slave named Bentura. Fearing a rebellion, the Dutch transferred the remaining slaves from Rincon to a stronghold near the saltpans called 'Tera Cora,' which means red soil. Bentura was eventually captured, although he later escaped to safety. Slavery was finally abolished in 1862.

During this period the Dutch had struggled to maintain possession of the colony. Twice at the beginning of the nineteenth century (1800-1803 and 1807-1815), the British captured Curacao, the capital of the Dutch West Indies, and thus gained control of Bonaire as well. They leased the island to Joseph Foulke, a North American ship-owner who exploited Bonaire as a source of lumber. When the islands were returned to the Netherlands by the Treaty of Paris of 1816, the small Fort Oranje was erected to guard against future attacks. It housed the island's commander until 1837, when it became a government depot and then a prison. Later, in 1868, a small lighthouse was built near Fort Oranje.

Although it lacked many of the resources that made other Caribbean colonies prosperous, Bonaire did have one precious commodity in great abundance--salt, which was a necessary ingredient for preserving meat and fish before refrigeration. In the late 1620's, when tensions heightened between Spain and its former principalities in the Netherlands, the Spanish had cut off the supply of this essential mineral to the Dutch. A few years later, when the Dutch captured Curacao, Bonaire, and Aruba, they gained valuable control of Bonaire's salt pans. Over the next two centuries the salt industry on Bonaire expanded, first under the Dutch West India Company and then under direct governmental control. By 1837 Bonaire's salt production had grown so large that four obelisks were built near the Salt Lake to guide ships coming in to load. The obelisks were painted red, white, blue, and orange (the colors of the Dutch flag and the Royal House of Orange), and a flag of one of the four colors would be raised high atop a flagpole to direct ships to the appropriate pan. In the middle of the nineteenth century, however, the salt industry on Bonaire fell into sharp decline, as the abolition of slavery and increased international competition sharply reduced its profitability. In 1870, the island's nine salt pans were purchased from the government by E.B.F. Hellmund. Today, they are operated by the Antilles International Salt Company.

With the end of slavery, Bonaire ceased to be a government plantation, and the land was put to public auction. Five plots, rich in lumber and in cattle, were sold in 1867 to J.F. Neuman & Co. and E.B.F. Hellmund (who later purchased the island's salt pans). The partitioning of property left the island's population disenfranchised and facing increasing poverty. Working for low wages, they lost even the sense of communal infrastructure they had possessed during slavery. Many left to take jobs in the copper mines in

Venezuela. Shortly after the turn of the century, the discovery of oil in Venezuela led to the development of refineries on Curacao and Aruba bringing new prosperity to the islands. Bonaire benefited as well, and a public works project was begun. The island blacktopped its roads, renewed the harbor, installed electricity and telephone connections, and improved medical conditions. The old lighthouse at Fort Oranje was replaced by a stone beacon in 1932, and an airport was built in 1936. During World War II, the island was an internment camp for captured Germans and Dutch Nazis. Wooden shacks confined 461 inmates between 1940 and 1947.

In 1936, Bonaire males were given the right to vote, and local political parties emerged over the next decade. It wasn't until after the war, however, that the islanders began to press for greater autonomy. Self-rule was granted by Queen Juliana of the Netherlands in 1954, although the Antilles remain a Dutch protectorate. Independence brought a greater emphasis on tourism. Bonaire, already a favorite of soldiers and officers, gained in popularity when Queen Juliana visited the island in 1944 with Eleanor Roosevelt. The Nazi internment camps were converted into the Hotel Zeebad, and the wooden shacks were replaced by charming stone bungalows. A second hotel, the Bonaire Beach Hotel, was opened up in 1962 on the Playa de Lechi. The Flamingo

Airport, originally constructed in 1955, was expanded in 1972 to support the increase in traffic. Seven years later Bonaire's Marine Park and Washington-Slagbaai Park were established, ensuring the survival of the island's extraordinary natural attractions well into the future.

Since 2010, Bonaire is considered a special municipality of the Netherlands together with Saba and Sint Eustatius and a part of the Dutch Caribbean.

Government

As of 10-10-'10 the Netherlands Antilles has ceased to exist. In the new constitutional structure, Curaçao and Sint Maarten have acquired the status of countries within the Kingdom (like the Netherlands Antilles and Aruba before the changes). Aruba retains the separate country status it has had since 1986. Thus, as from 10 October 2010, the Kingdom consists of four, rather than three, equal countries: Aruba, Curaçao and Sint Maarten are not Dutch overseas dependencies, but full, autonomous partners within the Kingdom, alongside the Netherlands, and each enjoys a high degree of internal autonomy.

The three other islands, Bonaire, Sint Eustatius and Saba have voted for direct ties with the Netherlands and are now part of the

Netherlands, thus constituting 'the Caribbean part of the Netherlands'. The relationship's legal form will be that each island has the status of public body within the meaning of article 134 of the Dutch Constitution. In broad terms, their position is now like that of Dutch municipalities, with adjustments for their small size, their distance from the Netherlands and their geographic situation in the Caribbean region. For the time being, Netherlands Antillean legislation will still be applicable in large part to the public bodies. Every resident of the three islands who has Dutch nationality now has the right to vote in elections to the Dutch House of Representatives alongside the existing right to vote in European Parliament elections. They are not, however, allowed to vote in Provincial Council elections because the public bodies are not part of any Dutch province.

The seat of the Netherlands Antilles government lies in Willemstad, Curacao. Bonaire and each of the other four islands within the association maintain control over internal affairs, but it is the central government based in Curacao that regulates police affairs, post, telecommunications, aviation, public health, and education, among others. The Netherlands Antilles government is based on a parliamentary democracy, and Parliament comprises a council of ministers and a prime minister. Bonaire, the second largets of all the Netherlands Antilles, comprises six distinct townships and villages. The island runs it's internal affairs through an elected legislative council, an advisory council, and executive council, comprising elected members of the island council. A lietenant governor, who is appointed by the queen, lives in Kralendijk and oversees local issues

National Symbols
Bonaire is part of the BES islands which forms part of the Dutch Caribbean. Although Bonaire is part of one country it still holds its own flag.

Description of the Bonaire flag
The flag contains the colors red-white –blue representing our respect for the Dutch Kingdom's tricolor.

At the upper end of our flag we have a yellow triangle, which is the bright light for our sun and also the beauty of our nature. Most Bonairean flowers are yellow like Kibrahacha, Kelki hel,Brasilia Hobada, Cucu, Sente-bibu, Anglo, Watapana and many others. The blue triangle is the color of our beautiful sea. Seen as a gigantic wave or a high mountain that we have to climb to reach the top for the progress of our nation.

The white symbolizes peace, liberty and tranquility. In the white area there is a black ring with four points of the navigation-compass. That compass is what our indisputable navigators have used to travel all over the world.

In the ring there is a six-pointed red star. The color symbolizes blood, as the fighting and surviving spirit of the six traditional regions which form together the people of Bonaire.

Coat of Arms of Bonaire

The crown; According to the heraldic regulations an island belonging to the Kingdom of the Netherlands has a right to carry the Duke's crown over its Coat of Arms.

The ships wheel; representing the Bonaireans who were always recognized as the best navigators (sailors) in the region. The compass-card and the star; the compass card symbolizes the determination to the course. The six pointed star represents the six traditional neighborhoods of Bonaire.

The blue color of the Coat of Arms; the blue color represents our unity with the sky and the sea, both are blue. The colors of the Caribbean Sea, which has always connected us to the rest of the world and which plays an important role in our economy.

Culture

Bonaire's Culture

Influences from around the world have been combined on Bonaire in a truly unique mixture, testifying to how successfully the people have been able to integrate their different ethnic Picture backgrounds. From Africa come the great festival dances of the Simadan and the Bari, with their polyphonic musicality and a whole range of percussive instruments.

The Bonairean culture is reflected in the faces of her people. Its origins are as varied as are the ethnic roots of the 15,000 plus residents. The real Bonairean culture is based on traditions that go back many generations and are chronicled in the songs and dances that are performed during holidays and festivals. It is also based on strong family ties and a general respect for nature and an understanding of an environment that originally was foreign to those first settlers and slaves that were forced to work the inhospitable, arid land.

Kids Those early days of slavery conditioned the people to be strong and to maintain a spirit that marks Bonaire and her people as extremely friendly and ready to smile when approached. Most of the people will raise a hand and wave to total strangers on the street. It was during this time that the spirit of the people began to develop and they made up songs, invented dances and began to sing in the old African Tradition. These songs and dances evolved into festivals and have survived to become an important part of life and culture on Bonaire.

Due to its somewhat mixed history and fortunes, the island's social heritage is particularly strong and incorporates elements from African, Caribbean and European influences. In the days of slavery, traditional African song and dance began to evolve, which are still extremely popular today. Dances such as the Mazurka and Polka are associated with the friendly people of Bonaire, while the European past can be seen in the architecture and cuisine.

The dances of the Simidan and the Bari are the best known. The traditional Waltz, Mazurka and the Polka and the local "Baile di Sinta" (ribbon dance) were performed as well as the Rumba, the

Carioca and Merengue which came from other islands. American Jazz also influenced the local traditions of song and dance. Along with an eclectic assortment of homemade musical instruments, those early performers set the stage for a rich, local tradition.

The culture of Bonaire can be seen in the faces of its people. The different features and hues tell the story of dozens of ethnic and racial influences. Indian, African, Asian and European inhabitants have all contributed to who Bonaire is today. Two of the most unmistakable features are the smiles that break out when greetings are made and the soft yet firm handshakes that pass between old and new friends.

Bonaire's culture is rooted in religious and holiday celebrations. Many traditions take origin from African homelands and European harvest and feast days. The music is a blend of tribal beats but using modern instruments and makeshift farming tools instead.

The Waltz, the Mazurka, the Polka, and a dance known locally as the 'Baile di Sinta,' which is something of a fertility dance performed around a maypole-all originate in Europe, as does the hand organ. The Rumba, the Carioca, and the Merengue migrated to Bonaire from the northern islands of the Caribbean, while Latin

America contributed the Danza and the Joropo. The United States provided its jazz rhythms.

Bonaire CultureThe harsh living conditions on Bonaire during slavery fostered a tremendous resilience in the spirit of the people and produced -- paradoxically -- much of the extraordinary liveliness and richness of Bonairean culture. To divert themselves while they worked, slaves took to singing in their native African styles. Over time, these work songs, unloading songs, filling-in songs, Saturday songs, and hammock songs (for the long day's end), developed into ritual festivities, complete with percussion instruments, vocal polyphony, and dancing.

Of particular note is the dance known as the Bari, which is still performed during the harvest festival of the same name, during the Simadan festival, and in the period following New Year's (Mascarada). The Bari is led by a solo singer who, very much like a Calypsonian, improvises satirical lyrics based on recent events and local figures. The soloist is accompanied by the beat of the Bari, a small drum covered in sheepskin and played like bongos. The dance is performed in two different and quite distinct stages. The first features the men, who compete with each other for the attention of the women-once a violent clash, this part of the Bari is today a highly stylized contest. In the second stage, the successful competitors get to dance with their choice of partners, though the couples never touch. The Tumba is a dance very similar in origin but more precisely choreographed. Its two sets, each consisting of eight steps, are accompanied by drums, while a variety of other instruments offer a complex polyphonic tune in place of the Bari soloist's lyrical inventions.

Musicians in Bonaire proved unusually resourceful in their ability to create new instruments from the discarded fragments of broken tools. A small percussive instrument known as the Chapi is made from the metal end of a hoe and is struck with a small metal bar. The blade of a plough serves as a base for the Agan, and the Simadan uses a scooped-out calabash floating in a tub of water. The Benta is a mouth-held string instrument made with a bowed-out knife. These, along with the cowhorn and the conch, form the traditional musical repertory of Bonaire.

Here is a sample of the traditional music as performed by "Tutti Frutti" a group of 17 singers from Rincon who preserve Bonairean musical heritage.

Simadan Festival

Sorghum harvest time in Bonaire is from February till the end of April. During this time the Kunuku (farm-owners), with the help of neighbors, friends and relatives, harvest the ripe and dry sorghum. To reward all this help and to celebrate the good harvest, a Simadan is set up at the Kunuku. It consists of dance, music, food, and abundant high spirits. The Simadan dance in Bonaire is called Wapa, which is a rhythmic, back-and-forth shuffle dance. Rows of people embrace, symbolizing the cooperative effort, and: Wapa!

Bonaire Siimadan FestivalSimadan has three traditional songs: Dan Simadan, Remailo, and Belua, all of which are sung in call-and-response form. The musicians use various typical instruments, including the marimba, wiri (guiro), bari (small drum), karko (empty conchshell -- strombus gigas linne), triangle, guitar, quarta (four-stringed guitar), and plain old hand-clapping.

Typical foods during Simadan include Funchi (similar to grits but less coarse) and Repa (pancakes made of Sorghummeal), served plain or with goat stew, goat soup, Giambo (okra soup, similar to gumbo), and Boontji Kunuku (local beans). All of these dishes are still an integral part of the Bonairean diet, although the availability of sorghummeal and boontji kunuku depends on the rainy season.

In the village of Rincon stands one of Bonaire's oldest and most symbolic buildings, the Mangasina di Rey, or Storehouse of the King. In earlier times, the building was the collective storage place for the island's food stores. During Simadan di Pastor, the culmination of the Simadan period, the area's kunuku-owners would bring a portion of their harvest to Rincon in celebratory processions, filled with song and dance. After the baskets of sorghum seed had been blessed at the church, and after prayers of thanks had been offered for the harvest, the seeds were given to the priest for storage in the Mangasina di Rey. During dry times, the community was supplied with sorghummeal. Simadan di Pastor, which takes place during Easter, is still celebrated in the towns of Nikiboko (on April 19) and Rincon (on April 20th).

Celebrations

This is what we do best. The traditional celebrations calendar in Bonaire is filled with exciting activities throughout the year. Most of these celebrations have some main elements in common, which is uniting people with food, music and dance. The celebrations on Bonaire are an important part of the culture on Bonaire. It's a form of reminding everyone that life is about having fun and dancing to the rhythm of the music.

Tradition

Being very resourceful, the people of Bonaire have combined their different ethnic backgrounds to produce a truly unique dance style. The rhythms are reminiscent of African drum beats yet contain modern influences making them seem fresh and new.

The Simadan, one of Bonaire's most widely known dances, is traditionally done in celebration of a successful maize harvest and takes place in fall. Everyone in the village plays a part in bringing in the crops and celebrating with food and drink.

The Bari is another Bonaire dance with harvest roots. It is strongly influenced by the Waltz, the Mazurka, the Polka, and a local dance 'Baile di Sinta,' which is performed around a maypole. These all originate in Europe. The Rumba, Carioca, and Meringue came to Bonaire from northern Caribbean islands, while Latin America contributed the Danza and the Joropo

Music & Instruments

The Bonaireans were quite resourceful in creating musical instruments. Of note was the Bari. It is a small rum barrel covered with a stretched sheepskin to create a drum. The Bari is used especially during the Simadan.

Many other instruments were fashioned from broken or discarded tools. The "Chapi" was a small percussive instrument made from the metal end of a hoe and struck with a small metal bar. A plow blade was used to make an Agan. For Simadan, a hollowed out calabash floating in a tub of water was used to tap out a beat. Conch shells and cow horns were valued instruments.

Local Artists

The Island is home to many accomplished artists from all over the world. Many genres are represented from around the world from fine art, fused glass, performance arts as well as poetry in the local language! Shops and galleries sell handcrafted items and paintings created by talented local artists.

A dried donkey jaw with teeth intact was used as a shaker creating a unique vibrational sound. Today, local musician Gaby Mercera creates and sells traditional instruments.

Traditional Dress

Owing to a warm climate, the early Bonaireans dressed in light colored cotton garments. The laborers wore mostly work clothes that served to protect them from the sometimes harsh elements. Head scarves, hats made from palm fronds and imported cloth were made into dresses and clothing for the families. Of course, when it came to dressing up for a festival or party, no expense was spared. The ladies turned out in fine dresses and the men wore suits and hats that were the fashion of the day.

Papiamentu

Papiamentu is a form of Creole indigenous to the Dutch Antilles, particularly Bonaire, Curacao, and Aruba, where it is considered the national language. It is also found in occasional use on Sint Maarten, Saba, and Statia. The term is a derivation of the old Spanish verb papear, which means to speak or converse.

Origins of the Language

Although there are numerous theories on the origins of Papiamentu, the most widely accepted explanation is that it is a Portuguese based Creole, traceable to the first contact between the Portuguese and West Africans in the mid-1400s. The Portuguese colonization of the West African coast prompted the evolution of a new language, one containing elements of African language structures and Portuguese vocabulary that allowed the two peoples to communicate with each other.

Bonaire's Papuamentu LanguageShortly thereafter, the Portuguese commenced the slave trade, shipping human cargo from the West African coast to the Americas. Gathered from all over West Africa, the slaves did not even share a common language, as they spoke dialects that varied considerably by region. To communicate with one another, as well as with the Portuguese, they slowly started to acquire the coastal Creole during the many months they were held in West African ports awaiting passage across the Atlantic. This lingua franca, which became the mother tongue of a new generation, evolved further as it was adapted to the particular linguistic environments in which the slaves found themselves. In many instances, the resulting Creole served as a secret language shared among the slaves, incomprehensible even to those owners who spoke Portuguese.

Evidence for this theory is found in the guene language, which was brought to Curacao by the first slaves to arrive on the island. Slaves would use it when they didn't want their shons (owners) to understand what they were saying. For a long time guene was neglected by linguists simply because it seemed incompatible with any potential root language. More recently, however, it was found to bear an unmistakable structural similarity to Crioulo, the Portuguese Creoles that are still spoken on the West African coast (in parts of Guinea Bissau, the Cape Verde Islands, Senegal, and Gambia). This resemblance suggests that guene is actually a remnant of the new language from the ports of West Africa, brought to Curacao around the 16th century. Other Portuguese based Creoles, all linked to early regions of Portuguese colonization, include Cafundo (in Brazil), Korlai (near Bombay, India), Macanese (in Hong Kong), Kristang (in Melaka, Malaysia), and Ternateno (in Maluku, Indonesia), and Indo-Portuguese (in Sri Lanka), although only Cafundo shares Papiamentu's West African origins.

Characteristics of Creole

Most nouns have no special form to indicate gender. Gender is created by adding the words homber (man)/machu (male) or muhe (woman) behind the noun: pushi machu - (cat male); mucha homber - (child male).

The nouns do not denote plurality when prefaced with a word with plural meaning: un homber - (one man); dos homber - (two men); un hende - (one person); hopi hende - (many people); un strea - (one star); tres strea - (three stars).

The verbs have no distinction of number: Ami ta bai - (I am going); Nos ta Bai - (We are going).

To indicate time and aspect, verbs use particles which stand on their own: Mi ta bai - (I am going); Mi tabata bai - (I was going); Mi lo bai - (I will go).

Most times the morpheme that indicates plurality has the same form as the third personal pronoun: nan - (they); muchanan - (children).

The presence of serial verbs: Sinta pensa (un ratu) - Sit and think (for a while); Lanta para wak - Stand up stand look.

Reduplication is used with different functions: pega-pega - (stick-stick) - a reptile that sticks to people; poko-poko - (slow-slow) - careful, very slow, annoyingly slow; tan-ten - (time-time) - in the meantime; pushi-pushi - (cat-cat) - quietly - as when a teenager is sneaking off to meet a date at 2 am.

A preference for the active voice rather than the passive: Nan ta ferf e kas - (They are painting the house); Nan ta straf e muchanan - (They are punishing the children).

Common Words & Phrases
Bon bini - welcome

Kon ta bai - hello

Bon dia - good morning

Bon tardi - good afternoon

Bon nochi - good evening

Si - yes

Danki - thank you

Dushi - sweetheart, sweet

Kome - eat

Bebe - drink

Drumi - sleep

Ayo - good-bye

Unda mi por kome kuminda krioyo? - (Where can I eat local food?)

Bo por mustra mi e kaminda pa Washington Park? - (Could you show me the way to Washington Park?)

Kon ta bai? - (How are you?)

E pomp di gasolin ta habri awor? - (Is the gas station open now?)

un, dos, tres, kuater, sinku, seis, shete, ocho, nuebe, djes - (1, 2, 3, 4, 5, 6, 7, 8, 9, 10)

Economy

Economy Over the years, Bonaire has developed an economy based on tourism, oil transference, salt production, and some light industry such as apparel manufacture and rice processing. By far, the oldest surviving industry on the island lies in the salt. Salt pans cover 10% of Bonaire's surface, and the island produces 441,000 tons (400,000 metric tons) per year. The Akzo Nobel Salt Company moved onto the island in 1963, and today it produces nearly half a million tons of salt at it's solar processing center (meaning after the salt is harvested and washed, it's dried by the sun) at Pekelmeer, at the southern tip of the island. This is the only spot today where salt is commercially produced. The salt harvest in rough grades used mainly for industry and ice-melting, rather than astable salt.

While Aruba and Curacao benefitted from the discovery of large quantities of oil in Venezuela in the early 20TH century, Bonaire did not. However, in 1975, the Bonaire Petroleum Corporation (BOPEC) was established. You'll see it today, at the northern end of the island near Gotomeer. The plant does not refine petroleum, but is a transfer center, stroing petroleum for transfer from large tankers to smaller ones.

The largest industry on Bonaire today is tourism. The 70,000 tourists who visit the island each year, a small number by Caribbean standards but just about right for Bonaire, contribute not only to direct sales such as hotel rooms and diving operators, but to related industries such as food and restaurants, retail sales, and transportation.

Tourism

Bon Bini

It is truly our pleasure to welcome you to Bonaire. An island blessed with an unsurpassed natural beauty.

From the depths of our pristine waters to the height of our tallest peak, Brandaris, you will feel Bonaire's magic wash over you from the moment you arrive and throughout the days as you become attuned to Bonaire's unhurried pace. You will find that, here on Bonaire, there is a peaceful ambiance for daily life, without the hassle of traffic lights, hustle and bustle, or normal, day-to-day worries. Your only concern will be how to spend each new day you have on Bonaire. Nowhere else is vacationing as easy as on Bonaire, as our warm, friendly people welcome visitors from around the world.

Next to other activities as, kite surfing, windsurfing and snorkeling, Bonaire continues to be recognized as one of the top destinations worldwide for its sustainable tourism. For the 24th consecutive year Bonaire was recognized as the number one Shore Diving Destination in the Caribbean/Atlantic in Scuba Diving Magazine's Annual Readers' Choice Awards. This year, it received 12 awards. It was also voted number one for Macro Diving and Beginner Diving.

Bonaire has a long history of nature preservation, and always seeks to find the delicate balance between environmental protection and growth, while maintaining nature and culture. Bonaire was one of the first Caribbean islands to collaborate with the Coral Restoration Foundation (CRF) to conserve our reefs. By commencing a program for cultivating new corals, specifically the stag horn and Elkhorn corals, Bonaire will be able to preserve the reef's genetic diversity. In this way residents, visitors and future generations will be able to enjoy an enriched marine environment.

But conservation and preservation is not limited to the marine environment. Bonaire continues to pursue initiatives that will reduce the CO_2 effects on our planet as we work towards fulfilling our promise to remain an 'Eco-Friendly' destination. Bonaire will continue to lead by example and strengthen its commitment to sustainable tourism practices.

We invite you to delve into the wonderful activities the island offers, both terrestrial and marine, which makes Bonaire a unique destination. We encourage you to explore, to enjoy, to become a part of Bonaire, absorbing our nature, our culture, and our cuisine. The warmth from the sunshine is here for all to enjoy while on Bonaire, but you will cherish the afterglow of the Bonairean people in your hearts forever. We assure you that "Once a Visitor Always a Friend".

Travel Guide

On an island with some of the world's most breathtaking coasts and coral reefs, it's no surprise that residents of Bonaire drive around with license plates proclaiming it's a "Diver's Paradise."

Tourists flock to the Caribbean island of Bonaire throughout the year to enjoy perfect diving and snorkeling conditions found along the coasts, in addition to the world-class windsurfing and boating opportunities. Inland, this Dutch municipality offers spectacular landscapes, which can be traversed on foot, horseback or bicycle. An impressive array of wildlife inhabits the area, including a large flamingo population and more than 190 species of birds.

Healthy portions of hospitality are served up around Bonaire, and despite its small size, a vast array of accommodation options can be found. Most of the hotels and guesthouses tend to be affiliated with diving schools and are fairly small, however, a number of high-end resorts have been springing up in recent years to cater to increasing numbers of tourists. The island is surprisingly renowned for its diverse cuisine, which is based on soups, stews and fish, in addition to Argentine, Italian and Chinese dishes. Most restaurants close for a few hours during the day for a siesta.

Although the island is world-famous for its spectacular diving and snorkeling, Bonaire has much more to offer. Day trips are popular and include excursions to the National Park, kayaking through the mangroves and land sailing on the world's longest track. There are also some enthralling walking tours, particularly in the quaint and historic towns of Rincon, the oldest village in Bonaire, and the capital, Kralendijk.

The most efficient way to traverse the island is on four wheels and it is possible to ship a car to Bonaire. However, it is much easier to rent one from the airport or your hotel. The island has also experienced a steady increase in its taxis over recent years, primarily due to Bonaire's growing popularity as a cruise port. An informal bus service, using vans, runs daily between the larger destinations, in addition to a few medium sized tour buses.

Highlights

✓ Dive off the coast to exploring some of the world's best reefs and corals.

✓ Go windsurfing in the choppy waters of Lac Bay, located in an 11 mile lagoon which offers perfect conditions.

✓ Hike the bucolic Washington-Slagbaai National Park, which is home to a plethora of wildlife including turtles, iguanas and birds of paradise.

✓ Stroll through the quaint capital, Kralendijk, taking in the sights, stopping for a drink and shopping for souvenirs.

✓ Sail from the Bay of Kralendijk in the early evening to enjoy a fantastic sunset.

✓ Visit the Lourdes Grotto shrine for a quiet moment of reflection.

✓ Gamble on the beach at the Caribbean's only barefoot casino at the Divi Flamingo Beach Hotel.

Travel Tips

Language

Dutch is the official language of Bonaire and is spoken by almost everybody; however, the native language is Papiamentu. Spoken exclusively on the ABC islands (Aruba, Bonaire and Curacao), Papiamento is a mix of Dutch, Spanish, Portuguese, Caribbean and African tounges. English is also widely spoken around the island and at tourist attractions.

Currency

Since January 2011, Bonaire has used the US dollar ($) as its official currency, with US $1 divided into 100 cents, but the Netherlands Antilles Guilder (NAFI) is still accepted everywhere. Currency can be exchanged at banks, airport and some hotels. ATMs are widely available, particularly at banks and shopping malls. Major credit cards are accepted in some establishments, but it's always best to check for your card supplier's mark before trying to make a purchase. Travelers' checks can be exchanged at banks with proper proof of identity.

Time

The island is on Atlantic Standard Time, which is either three or four hours behind GMT (GMT -3/-4), depending on Daylight Saving Time.

Electricity

Bonaire uses electricity at 220V with Europlug and Schuko plug sockets. Visitors wishing to use electrical appliances that operate according to a different voltage in Bonaire will need a transformer, while appliances that have different plugs to the region's Type B plugs will need a plug adaptor. Most US appliances do not require an adaptor.

Communications

The dialing code for Bonaire is +599. Purchasing a SIM card is straightforward and major local networks are Digicel and CHIPPIE. Most of the island has mobile phone coverage. Internet cafes are rather infrequent outside of the capital city, although most resorts have wireless service, usually for a fee.

Duty-free

Duty-free alcohol, cosmetics, perfume and other items are available to international passengers at Flamingo International Airport. Customs allowances depend on the country you're entering, with passengers able to purchase up to 400 cigarettes, two liters of distilled beverages and two liters of wine from the duty-free store.

Weather

Due to its fortunate position on the equator, Bonaire enjoys one of the Caribbean's most pleasant climates. with very little rainfall (less than 22 inches annually) and a prevailing easterly trade wind that provides a constistent 15 mph (= 25 Kmh) breeze. This trade wind is also one of the coral reefs best friends and a major reason these reefs are among the most prolific in the world. When the wind blows constinuously from the same direction, one side of the island has "rough" water conditions (the windward side), the other side (the leeside) is almost always clam. Since Bonaire lies at a 90 degree angle to its trade winds, the island's western side (where you'll find all of the snorkeling operations) is always calm and protected.

Not only does this provide perfect snorkeling conditions about 99% (no exaggeration) of the time, it also alows corals to grow prolifically in shallow water (rough water tends to knock some of the corals over, preventing them from attaining full growth). The low rainfall on Bonaire is also a blessing, since fresh water from rivers (there are no rivers on Bonaire) and rain runoff are enemies of the coral reef. Freshwater runoff almost contains sediments, which can harm the coral by literally smothering it.

The temperature is extremely consistent throughout the years, ranging from 79°F to 89°F with an average temperature of 81.5°F. Rainfall is few and far between, with less than 22 inches annually, which greatly benefits diving and snorkeling conditions. In fact, the western side of the island is always calm due to Bonaire's location at a 90 degree angle, while the trade winds on the eastern side rarely exceed 15 mph. Although Bonaire's almost perfect weather conditions are extremely appealing, visitors should bear in mind that protection from the sun is still essential so always bring sunscreen and hats. Located just under the hurricane belt, tropical storms are unlikely to dampen your trip.

Best Time to Visit Bonaire

Bonaire is an ideal destination to visit year-round due to its consistent good weather. Even in the brief rainy season, travelers will not be disappointed. There are a range of activities especially off the coast where the coral reef thrives because of the perfect climate. The island experiences a steady flow of visitors throughout the year, particularly between October and April when North Americans are looking to escape the harsh winters back home. Make sure to book accommodation well in advance if planning a trip during this period. February is the busiest month as a result of Carnival, the biggest festival of the year. The majority of establishments and attractions are open year-round, especially now that cruise ships dock on the island almost daily. If you want your experience on Bonaire to be tranquil and uninterrupted, the low season is a great time to visit the bucolic island and take advantage of cheap hotel and dive deals.

Visas and Vaccinations

Citizens of the UK, Germany, Spain and several others do not require a visa to stay in Bonaire for up to 90 days, while residents of The Netherlands, Belgium and Luxembourg do not even need a passport to enter the country. Nationals of the US, Australia and Canada can stay on the island for up to two weeks without a visa. Passports must be valid for at least six months upon arrival. Travelers from other countries should check their visa requirements at http://www.infobonaire.com/entryrequirements.html.

Health and Safety

Very little crime is reported in Bonaire; however, the usual precautions are always worth keeping in mind. Try to avoid traveling alone at night and avoid carrying valuables or large amounts of money. There are few signs of poverty and locals tend to be extremely friendly. Attacks against tourists are almost unheard of; however, it always helps to keep an eye on belongings, especially in large crowds. Valuables should not be left unattended on the beach or in hotel rooms and always use the safety deposit box.

Tap water and the local food are both fine for consumption. It is always worth investing in private healthcare before visiting Bonaire as medical offices are not few and far between. The island's only hospital, the 60-bed Hospitaal San Francisco in Kralendijk, has comprehensive emergency facilities. Vaccinations are not necessary and Malaria and Yellow Fever are not an issue. If medication is required, pharmacies can found throughout the capital in some smaller communities, usually keeping standard hours.

Transportation

Bonaire Taxis and Car Rental

Taxis are the only form of public transportation on the island and are a fairly inexpensive way to explore Bonaire. Most drivers speak good English and are usually held to a high-standard. Taxi 14 Kenneth and Katharina (+599-700-3026) and Taxi # 9 Christie Dovale (+599-795-3456) are both well known local companies.

Car rental is available on the island and is a great way to get around, however, the driver must have a valid license from the US, Canada or Europe. Vehicles can be rented primarily from the airport and in downtown Kralendijk. Local firm, Bonaire Rent a Car (+599-786-6090) offers competitive rates and is a popular choice. Motorbikes and mopeds are also available for hire through Rento Fun Drive (+599-717-2408). The roads are clearly marked and driving is done on the right hand side of the road. Adhere to the speed limits because a donkey or goat in the middle of the road may surprise you.

Bonaire Water Taxis

Twice daily water taxis run between Bonaire and nearby Klein Bonaire, leaving from the main pier. Water taxi is the only way to reach this tiny island unless you rent a boat. The trip is an extremely pleasant experience and great daytrip with gentle music playing while you knock back a couple of cold ones en route.

Bonaire Boat Rental

Renting a private boat is a fantastic way to traverse the coastline of Bonaire and Klein Bonaire at you own leisure. They can be borrowed for half a day or full day through Blue Bay Rentals (+599-701-5500).

Food and Restaurants

The cuisine of Bonaire, like that of many islands of the Caribbean, brings together the myriad influences of the many cultures and people who made the island's history. The resulting culinary palette is a colorful one, incorporating the zesty cooking of Sephardic Jews from Spain and Portugal, robust northern European fare imported from Holland, exotic Indonesian spices which reached the island via the maritime traffic of the Dutch Empire, and bold, flavorful cooking carried to Bonaire from West Africa.

Although Bonaire's many constituent cultures brought unusual diversity to its cuisine, the island's limited capacities for agricultural production encouraged cooks to adapt their recipes to the particular range of ingredients available here. Although imports from abroad were sporadic, residents created a wide range of dishes--from soups and stews to sweets and desserts. Many of these dishes rely on easily preserved staples such as salted meat (which kept longer in pre-freezer days), some on such mainstays of Caribbean cooking as plantains and okra, and others on the unique bounty of Bonaire's environment-including cactus and iguana.

Bonaire's cuisine is considerably varied as a result of the cultural diversity of the inhabitants. Seafood is naturally a common theme on many restaurant menus, with the most popular dishes including conch shell meat, lobster and grilled spicy fish, in addition to stews and soups. Most of the island's eateries are located in the capital and are wide-ranging in terms of style and standard. Even though the island doesn't actually raise any of its own food products, the variety of cuisines available is vast. Most of the bars are located in Kralendijk and tend to stay open until around midnight.

Bars and Pubbing in Bonaire
As with most destinations in the Caribbean, nightlife is a laid-back and carefree affair. Happy hours are the norm and cocktails, in addition to Dutch beers such as Amstel and Heineken, are often found at bars. In Kralendijk, C'est La Vie Bonaire Bar (Kaya Simon L

Bolivar 21, Kralendijk) has gained quite a reputation in recent years for its friendly atmosphere, delicious cocktails and reasonable prices. Another popular spot is the Paradise Moon Bar and Restaurant (Kaya Korsou 1, Kralendijk), located on the coastline, making it a great place to catch the sunset. Just along the waterfront is the infamous City Cafe Bonaire (Kaya Grandi 7, Kralendijk), which has been operating for more than 15 years. It is perhaps the island's best live music venue and stays open relatively late most nights.

The cozy town of Rincon is Bonaire's oldest settlement and houses some of the island's most authentic bars, such as the Posada Para Mira (Kaya Para Mira, Rincon). Located in the hills on the way to Dos Pos, the place comes to life on weekends with the sound of festive music. Overlooking Lac Bay, Kon Tiki Beach Bonaire (Kaminda Sorobon 64, Lac Bay) is a charming cocktail bar which offers spectacular views of the lagoon and boasts year-round art exhibitions. For an authentic beach party, check out Karels Beach Bar (Kaya J N E Craane 12, near Harbour Village), a place where cool tunes and booze are always flowing.

Dining and Cuisine in Bonaire
Bonaire is home to around 80 restaurants, most of which are located in and around Kralendijk. One of the most renowned is the

Playa Krioyo Restaurant Bonaire (Kaya Isla Riba 1, Kralendijk), which serves up traditional local favorites, such as sopi kabrito (goat soup) and baka stoba (beef stew). Open only on the weekend, the delicious Bobbejan BBQ (Kaya Albert Engelhardt 2, Kralendijk), centered in the heart of the capital and offers some of the best grilled meats on the island. Lilly's Ice Cream Shop (Kaya L D Gerhards 5, Kralendijk), one of the most established joints, quite rightly claims to make some of the best ice cream in the Caribbean, while the coffee is also outstanding.

If you are headed from Rincon to Washington Slagbaai National Park, be sure to stop at LeMaSe Restaurant (Kaya Rincon 34, Rincon), a quaint villa offering homemade treats from local soups to tasty milkshakes. El Fogon Latino Restaurant (Kaya Nikiboko Zuid 88, Lac Bay) in perhaps the island's best South American restaurant, serving primarily Colombian dishes that are well worth checking out after a day exploring the Lac Bay lagoon.

Many of the hotels and restaurants in Bonaire serve native island fare, but these dishes may not appear on the menu, so be sure to ask about unlisted specials.

For those, who are vegetarian, most restaurants will have vegetarian options or will accommodate your requests.

Dining & Restaurants
B: Breakfast, L: Lunch, D: Dinner

Ocean View

Restaurant		Phone Prefix +599		Food Style
4 Seasons	Kaya CEB Hellmund 17	717-4166	D	International
At Sea	Kaya C.E.B. Hellmund 25	701-0134	D	International
City Restaurant	Kaya J.N.E. Craane	717-8286	B,L,D	Pasta or green salads, sandwiches, sushi, or hot food
It Rains Fishes	Seaside	717-8780	D	International
Ingridients	Buddy Dive	717-1684	D	International
Karel's Beach Bar Cappuccino Bar	Seaside	717-8434		- reggae, soca, and dancing
La Barca Bar Restaurant	Oceanfront Promenade	717-4514 or 795-	D	Italian

		1932		
La Guernica Fish & Tapas	Kaya Bonaire 4c	717-5022	D	Seafood, tapas
La Luna	Kaya C.E.B. Hellmund 17	717-2370	L,D	Variety
Paradise Moon	Kaya Korsow 1	717-5025	D	Interntional
Tipsy Seagull	Plaza Resort	717-2500	D	Variety
Wattaburger	Oceanfront Promenade	717-3547	L,D	Fast Food
Zeezicht Seaside Restaurant	Kaya J.N.E. Craane 12	717-8434	B,L,D	Variety/Local

Local Cuisine

Restaurant		Phone Prefix +599		Food Style
Antriol Catering	Kaya Mariana 8	717-4248	L, D	Local

Divi Divi Restaurant	Kaya Dr. J.G. Hernandez 26	717-6975	L,D	Local
Gibis	Kaya Hulanda	09-567-0655		Local
KishiKishi Lunch Cafe	At the Butterfly Farm	795-8989	L	Incorporates foods produced locally
Maiky's Snack	Kaminda Nieuw Amsterdam 30	09-567 0078	D	Local
Playa Krioyo	Kaya Isla Riba 1	717-3997	L,D	Local
Posada Para Mira Open weekends	Rincon	701-7060	L,D	Local
Rose Inn	Rincon	717-6420	B,L,D	Local
Slagbaai Beach Bar & Restaurant Casual dining. Open daily from 11 until 4:00 PM	Washington Slagbaai National Park		L	Local
Verona's Bar Restaurant	Kaya Para Mira 2 (Rincon)	717-6440	L,D	Local

Continental Cuisine

Restaurant		Phone Prefix +599		Food Style
4 Seasons	Kaya CEB Hellmund 17	717-4166	D	International
Banana Tree	Plaza Resort	717-2500	L,D	Variety
El Mundo	Kaya Grandi 7	717-4601	B,L,D	International
La Luna	Kaya C.E.B. Hellmund 17	717-2370	L,D	Variety
E Terras	Kaya Nikiboko Zuid #8	717-4141	L,D	Local and international food
The Caribbean Club Restaurant and Bar	at Caribbean Club	717-7901	L,D	Local Cuisine, International Wines and Bar
Kontiki Beach Club	Lac Bay Resort	717-5369	B,L,D	Variety, Jazz night
The Pool Bar & Restaurant	at Buddy Dive Resort	717-5080	B,L,D	International

Pzazz Beach Club Restaurant	Sorobon Beach Resort	717-8080	B,L,D	Salads, sandwiches, and other beachfare
Spice Beach Club	Eden Beach Resort	717-8060	B,L,D	International
Roomer Hotel Restaurant	E.E.G. Boulevard 97, Belnem	717-7488	B,D	Variety
Zeezicht Seaside Restaurant	Kaya J.N.E. Craane 12	717-8434	B,L,D	Variety/Local

Tapas and Light Fare

Restaurant		Phone Prefix +599		Food Style
C'est La Vie	Across from the Catholic Church in Kralendijk	788-1066	D	Dutch pub, with daily barhop menu
Little Havana	Kaya Bonaire 4	786-0717		Tapas, Bar
Yacht Club Lounge & Tapas Bar	Kaya Gob. N. Debrot 54	782-3550	D	Tapas

La Guernica Fish & Tapas	Kaya Bonaire 4c	717-5022	D	Seafood, tapas

bonairetalk.com

Restaurant		Phone Prefix +599		Food Style
Bistro de Paris	Harbour Village Marina	717-7070	L,D	Authentic French and International
Donna & Giorgio's	Kaya Grandi 52	717-3799	B,L,D	Breakfast and lunch Monday through Friday; dinner by reservation only on Tuesdays and Fridays
It Rains Fishes	Seaside	717-8780	D	International
Mona Lisa Bar & Restaurant	Kaya Grandi 15	717-8718	L,D	Variety
Paradise Moon	Kaya Korsow 1	717-	D	International

		5025		
Plazita Limena	Kaya Grandi 6	717-7667	B,L,D	Peruvian and International
Unbelievable	Kaya J. A. Abraham Boulevard 29	717-3000	D	International
Wil's Tropical Grill	Kaya L. D. Gerharts #9	717-6616	D	Continental

Bonaire Talk Honorable Mention

Restaurant		Phone Prefix +599		Food Style
At Sea	Kaya C.E.B. Hellmund 25	701-0134	D	International
Bobbejan's weekends only	Kaya Albert Engelhardt 2	717-4783	L,D	BBQ
Capriccio	Kaya Hellmund	717 7230	L,D	Fine Italian food, excellent

Ristorante	#5			desserts
Chibi Chibi	Divi Flamingo Beach Resort	717-8285	L, D	International
El Fogon Latino	Kaya Nikiboko Zuid 88	717-2677	L,D	Colombian
Jibe City Hang Out Bar	Kaya Sorobon	717-5064	L	Beach bar
La Balandra	Harbour Village Beach Club	717-7500	L	International
Mi Banana	Kaya Nikiboko Noord 42C	717-4472	L,D	Colombian/International
Rum Runners	Capt. Don's Habitat	717-7303	B,L,D	Variety

Top 9 Rated by Trip Advisor

Restaurant		Phone Prefix +599	Food Style	

Appetite	Kaya Grandi 12	717-3595	L,D	International
At Sea	Kaya C.E.B. Hellmund 25	701-0134	D	International
Bistro de Paris	Harbour Village Marina	717-7070	L,D	Authentic French and International
Capriccio Ristorante	Kaya Hellmund #5	717-7230	L,D	Fine Italian food, excellent desserts
Pasa Bon Pizza	Kaya Gob N Debrot	780-1111	D	Pizza
Paradise Moon	Kaya Korsow 1	717-5025	D	International
Rumba Cafe	Harbourside Mall	717-8298	B,L,D	Variety
Unbelievable	Kaya J. A. Abraham Boulevard 29	717-3000	D	International
Wil's Tropical Grill	Kaya L. D. Gerharts #9	717-6616	D	Continental

Best Wine List

Restaurant		Phone Prefix +599		Food Style
Capriccio Ristorante	Kaya Hellmund #5	717-7230	L,D	Fine Italian food, excellent desserts

Breakfast Buffet

Restaurant		Phone Prefix +599		Food Style
Calabas Restaurant	Divi Flamingo Beach Resort	717-8285	B	Breakfast buffet

BBQ, Grill & Ribs

Restaurant		Phone Prefix +599		Food Style
Beach Hut	Kaya Sorobon at Bonaire Windsurf	717-7288	L	Beach bar

	Place	or 701-6500		
Bobbejan's weekends only	Kaya Albert Engelhardt 2	717-4783	L,D	BBQ,
Bonaire Grill	Parking Lot of Post Office	786-6212 or 796-6212	D	Grill truck for ribs and chicken
Cactus Blue	JA Abraham Blvd 12	717 4564	D	International and Food Truck at "Atlantis" Kite Beach
Dive Hut Restaurant	Kaya Dialama	701-0404	L,D	Various Swiss Theme Nights
Eddy's Restaurant at Sand Dollar	Kaya Gob. N. Debrot	788-0128	B,L	Breakfast buffet, Lunch and Afternoon Snacks, Friday night BBQ Buffet
Gibis	Kaya Hulanda	09-567-0655		

Ribs Factory	Harbourside Mall, 2nd floor		D	Ribs, Grill

Steaks

Restaurant		Phone Prefix +599		Food Style
Grill House	Kaya J.N.E. Craane 12	717-8434	D	Grill
Hilltop	At Caribbean Club	717-7901	L,D	Grill, International, Bar
Patagonia Steak House	Kaya Grandi	717-7725	D	Argentinean Steak House
Plazita Limona	Kaya Grandi 6	717-7667	B,L,D	Peruvian and International

Fast Food

Restaurant		Phone Prefix +599		Food Style
Kentucky Fried Chicken	36 Kaya Korona	717-7700	L,D	Fast food
Het Flaamse Frits Huis	Kaya Korona 69		L,D	Flemish Fries House
Subway	Les Galleries Kaya L.D. Gerharts	717-2110	B,L,D	Fast food
Wattaburger	Oceanfront Promenade	717-3547	L,D	Fast Food

Chinese

Restaurant		Phone Prefix +599		Food Style
Bon Appetit	Gilberto F. Croes 10	717-7371	L,D	Chinese
China Nobo	Kaya A.A. Emerenciana 4	717-8981	L,D	Cantonese

Dragon City	Kaya Gob. N. Debrot	717-3188	L,D	Chinese
Enping Bar Restaurant	Kaya S. Bolivar	717-4422	L,D	Chinese
Fareast Bar & Restaurant	Kaya Avelino J Cecilia	717-7177	L,D	Chinese
Great China	Kaya Grandi 39	717-8886	L,D	Chinese
Jos Bar Restaurant	Kaya Korona 79	717-6600	L,D	Chinese
Mentor Bar & Restaurant	Kaya Korona 140	717-4999	L,D	Chinese
New Wei Taai	Kaya A.J. Cecilia 31	717-2127	L,D	Surinam and Chinese
Peking Bar Restaurant	Kaya Tintorero 1	717-7170	L,D	Chinese
Shang Hai Bar Restaurant	Kaya L.D. Gerharts 17	717-8838	L,D	Chinese
Spanhoek	Kaya L.D. Gerharts	717-6686	L,D	Suriname
Surinaamse Bar	Kaya A. Cecillia 31	717-2127	L,D	Suriname

Restaurant				
Yue Hau Restaurant	Papa Cornes 33	717-2180	L,D	Chinese

Italian

Restaurant		Phone Prefix +599		Food Style
Capriccio Ristorante	Kaya Hellmund #5	717-7230	L,D	Fine Italian food, excellent desserts
La Barca Bar Restaurant	Oceanfront Promenade	717-4514 or 795-1932	D	Italian
Pasa Bon Pizza	Kaya Gob N Debrot	780-1111	D	Pizza

Ice Cream and Desserts

Restaurant		Phone Prefix	Food Style

		+599		
Gio's	Kaya Grandi	717-5700		Homemade ice cream, pastries, coffee, chocolats, bon-bons
Lamase Soda Fountain	Kaya Rincon 34, Rincon	717-6343		Soda fountain
Lilly's Ice Cream & Coffee	Kaya L.D. Gerharts 5	795-3747		Ice Cream and Coffee
Lovers Ice Cream	Sand Dollar Mall	717-5738	L,D	Ice Cream, Yogurt, Hot dogs Surinam Food

Deli

Restaurant		Phone Prefix +599		Food Style
Between 2 Buns	Sand Dollar Plaza	705-4709	B,L	Deli

Boudoir Food & Drinks	Kaya Grandi 26F-G	717-4321	Deli/Sandwiches

Japanese Cuisine

Restaurant		Phone Prefix +599		Food Style
Osaka Sushi Bar	Kaya Grandi 52-		B,D	Sushi

Café

Restaurant		Phone Prefix +599		Food Style
Brandaris Cafe	Kaya Libertador Simon Bolivar 22	717-4596	B,L,D	Sandwiches, Coffee, Local Food
City Restaurant	Kaya J.N.E. Craane	717-8286	B,L,D	Pasta or green salads, sandwiches, sushi, or hot food

Mondrian Restaurant	Kaya L.D. Gerharts	717-1210	B,L	Breakfast, Lunch and Coffee

Cooking School

Restaurant		Phone Prefix +599		Food Style
Chez Nous	Comprehensive School call for reservations	717-8120	L,D	Caribbean

At the Airport

Restaurant		Phone Prefix +599		Food Style
Restaurant Le Mirage	At the Flamingo Airport	717-5600 x231	B,L,D	Variety
Techno Bar	At the Flamingo Airport	717-7716	B,L,D	Variety

		or 717-7717		

Other Choices

✓ See the sunset from aboard the Siamese Junk Samur or aboard the Trimaran Woodwind.

✓ Night dives, especially at the town pier (please check with dive shop for permission.

✓ There are many slide shows and lectures various nights of the week at resorts. Check the Update flyer for more info.

✓ On weekends, many of the Ranchos (local ranches) have live bands and local cuisine, and open their doors to both locals and tourists.

✓ Don't forget to check out the Flamingoes at sunset from Pekelmeer. Be sure to bring your binoculars or telephoto lens.

✓ Take a "Tuk tuk" tour.

✓ Try a night snorkel with Renee Snorkel Trips or H2O Visions Snorkel Tours.

Recipes

The following recipes give a good introduction to the tastes and variety of this Caribbean island. Because they are featured in Bonairean festivals, and because they are among the most interesting Bonairean dishes, we have included rather more soups than other dishes. All of the recipes are derived from This is the Way We Cook! (asina nos ta cushinà): Recipes from the outstanding cooks of the Netherlands Antilles, compiled by Jewell Fenzi with illustrations by Helen Dovale. As they say in Bonaire, Bon Probecho (Bon Appetit)!

Pastechis (4 dozen)

The versatile pastechi is a plump, little pastry filled with spicy meat, shrimp or fish. It appears everywhere, around the clock: with coffee, tea or cocktails, at beach parties, or on the most formal buffet tables.

Filling: Rub with the juice of several limes 1 lb. chicken breasts and 1 lb. chicken thighs. Season the breast and thighs with salt and pepper, poultry seasoning and minced onion. Let stand for several hours, then arrange the pieces in a shallow baking dish. Brown the chicken under the broiler, then bake for one hour at 350 degrees, deboning and chopping it when cool.

Dough: Sift and set aside 6 cups flour. Cream 3 heaping tablespoons butter, 3 heaping tablespoons shortening, 1 1/2 tablespoons salt and 2 small eggs. Add 2 cups of the flour to the shortening mixture. Add, a little at a time, 1 1/2 cups water. Continue adding flour two cups at a time until it is absorbed in the mixture. When the dough is pliable, knead it well.

Roll the dough into a very thin sheet, then cut out circles about 3 inches in diameter. Place one tablespoon filling in the center of one pastry circle. Top it with a second circle. Lightly moisten edges and press the circles together. Fold or roll the edges over slightly and flute them as with pie crust. Fry the pastechis in deep, hot fat until golden brown. They may be prepared in advance and heated in the oven just before serving.

Sòpi di Binja (serves 10-12)
This wine soup is an Antillean favorite.

In a large saucepan, bring 6 cups of water to a rapid boil and add 30 prunes and one or two cinnamon sticks. Reduce the heat and simmer prunes until soft. Remove the saucepan from the fire and permit it to cool. Discard the cinnamon sticks and remove the prunes from the liquid, setting them aside for later use.

Stir into the cooled liquid 1/2 cup cornstarch, mixed with enough water to make a smooth paste. Return the saucepan to a low flame, and stir the liquid until it thickens. Add 2 one-fifth bottles dry red wine and 3/4 cup sugar and bring to a boil. Stir until the sugar is dissolved. The soup should have body and a smooth consistency. If it is too thick, add water a little at a time. Add the prunes just before serving.

Sòpi di Yuwana, or Iguana Soup (Serves 6-8)

Small boys in the countryside, or kunuku snare yuwana, or iguana, and offer them for sale along the roadsides. Choose a plump one for this delicacy, which tastes a bit like rabbit and a little like chicken.

Clean, skin, and cut into serving pieces one iguana. Place in a heavy kettle 1 & 1/2 quarts water, 2 chicken bouillon cubes, 1 clove garlic, 1 leek, 1 tomato (coarsely chopped), 1 onion (studded with 3 cloves), 1 green pepper (quartered), 1/4 of a small cabbage.

Bring to a boil, reduce heat and simmer for thirty minutes. Ad the iguana, and simmer an additional half hour, or until the meat is tender. Remove from the fire. Strain the broth, discarding the vegetables. Bone the iguana and set the meat aside.

Return the broth to the fire and add 1 teaspoon cumin (or to taste), a dash of nutmeg, salt and pepper, and a few ounces of vermicelli. Simmer for about five minutes until the vermicelli is tender. Add the iguana and heat thoroughly. Serve piping hot with funchi.

Giambo (Okra Soup) Serves 6-8

Giambo (pronounced ghee-Yam-bo) is the traditional Antillean gumbo. A thick, hearty soup, it is a traditional dish of the Simadan festivities. The purèed okra gives it a slippery consistency.

Soak overnight 1/2 lb. salted beef. Discard the water, and place the beef in a heavy kettle with 2 quarts of fresh water, 1 ham hock, 1-2 onions, a few sprigs of parsley, 1-2 carrots, 1 bay leaf, 1 celery stalk. Bring to a brisk boil. Reduce heat and simmer for about one and a half hours, or until the meat is tender.

Place in the simmering kettle 1 lb. red snapper fillets. After a few minutes test the fish with the tines of a fork, and remove them from the broth when the meat flakes easily. Cut the fish into bite-sized pieces. Remove the beef from the broth, cube and set aside with the fish. Strain the broth and return it to the fire.

Discard the ham hock and vegetables. To the simmering broth add 2 lbs. okra (washed and sliced), a few sprigs crushed yerba di hole (or fresh basil), 1/2 teaspoon black pepper. Simmer until the okra is tender. With a wire whisk, reduce the okra to a pure(accent)e. Return the cubed beef and red snapper pieces to the kettle. Heat thoroughly and adjust seasonings. Garnish giambo with 1/4 lb. cooked shrimp. Funchi is a must with this delicious soup.

Island Curry (serves 8)

Place in a heavy kettle: 1 large chicken (about 5 pounds), 2 celery sticks, 1 or 2 onions (studded with several cloves), 4 cups water, 3 sprigs parsley, 2 teaspoons salt. Simmer for one half-hour or more, until the chicken is tender. Strain the stock and return it to the kettle. When the chicken is cool enough to handle, remove the meat in large chunks and set aside. Return the chicken bones and skin to the stock. Add one cup of water and simmer the stock for an additional 45 minutes. Strain the stock a second time and set it aside. There should be at least four cups. Up to this point, the preparations may be made a day in advance.

When it is time to make the curry, use a large, heavy kettle to sauté: 5 tablespoons butter, 4 onions coarsely chopped, 1 large apple (peeled and chopped). Stir the onions and apple frequently until they are translucent, but not browned. Remove them from the pan, pressing out the butter as it is needed for the sauce base.

Blend in 4 tablespoons flour. Continue stirring until the flour and butter are slightly browned. Remove the kettle from the fire and permit it to cool slightly. Add the chicken broth, then return the kettle to the fire. Stir the sauce constantly until it is smooth and thick.

Add 1 cup raisins, juice of half a lemon and a strip of lime peel. Simmer the sauce an additional five minutes, then add 1 cup light cream. Add 2 teaspoons curry powder, mixed with a little water. Taste, then add more seasoning until the sauce is spicy. Antilleans may use as many as five tablespoonfuls!

Remove the strip of lime peel, then add the chicken pieces, the sautéed onions, and apple to the sauce. Warm the sauce only until the chicken is heated through, but do not boil it. Serve the curry over rice, with any combination of the following ingredients: chopped hard-boiled eggs, peanuts, fresh grated coconut, diced bananas, minced green pepper or chutney.

Funchi (serves 6)

Funchi is an Antillean staple, often served with soup.

Mix in a heavy saucepan: 1 1/4 cups cold water, 1 1/2 cups corn meal, 1 teaspoon salt. Stir in: 1 1/2 cups boiling water, 1 tablespoon butter.

Bring to a brisk boil over high heat and cook for three minutes. Continue cooking an additional three minutes, stirring the funchi vigorously with a wooden spoon.

When the mixture is very stiff and pulls away from the sides of the pan, remove from the fire. Turn out into a deep, well-buttered bowl and cover with a plate. Shake the funchi down into the bowl, then invert it on a serving platter.

For a special Sunday breakfast, fry sliced funchi in butter and serve with crisp bacon and scrambled eggs.

Cocada (about 3 cups)

Traditionally, this coconut candy is served on broken bits of a coconut shell.

In a saucepan, combine: 1 lb. brown sugar and 1 cup water. Simmer gently until the mixture forms a thick syrup. Have a cup of cold water ready. Drop a little of the boiling syrup into it.

When the syrup can be gathered up in the fingers as a soft ball, remove the saucepan from the fire. Stir in immediately: 1 lb. fresh grated coconut, and juice of half a lime. Turn out onto a lightly buttered platter and spread to cool.

Airports

Flamingo International Airport

Situated close to Bonaire's capital, Flamingo International Airport is the third largest in the former Netherlands Antilles, receiving more than 21,000 passengers a year. The original airport opened in 1945 and was upgraded in the 1950's. In addition to a variety of connections to nearby islands, the airport has flights to a number of major European and North American cities, such as Miami and Amsterdam. The most popular airlines are local carriers Dutch Antilles Express and EZAir, for which Flamingo International is a hub, in addition to KLM, Delta Air Lines and United Airlines.

There's a range of dining options, bars and a recently updated departure hall, in addition to a few duty-free stores. Car rental through major international chains Avis and Hertz, and local firms is available, and there's always a number of taxis waiting outside. Further plans to upgrade the facility in coming years are in place to accommodate the growing tourist arrivals.

Queen Beatrix International Airport (Aruba)

The Netherlands Antilles largest airport, Queen Beatrix International Airport welcomed more than 1 million passengers in 2011. The one terminal facility has direct and connecting flights to various destinations worldwide. About 30 airlines fly from Aruba, the most active being United Airlines, Gol Transportes Aereos and

Avior Airlines. In recent years, the busiest routes have been to New York, Miami and Newark. The terminal has a good selection of restaurants, fast-food chains, bars and duty-free stores. Transfers to Bonaire's Flamingo International are commonplace, and it is also possible to travel by sea. All major car rental companies are present at the airport, in addition to taxis and bus services.

Simon Bolivar International Airport of Maiquetia (Venezuela)

Located about 13 miles outside the capital city of Caracas, Simon Bolivar Airport is the main gateway to Venezuela with almost 10 million travelers passing through in 2011. Due to its proximity to the ABC Dutch Antilles, this airport is a popular option for long haul arrivals who find it more practical to connect from here to Bonaire in the Southern Caribbean. The airport has two terminals, both of which include a variety of duty-free stores, restaurants and bars. Major airlines flying from Caracas include Aserca Airlines, Conviasa and RUTACA Airlines.

Attractions

Languishing in the Caribbean Ocean not far from the coast of Venezuela, Bonaire has maintained an air of seclusion and visitors come here throughout the year to soak up the sunshine and sea. However, there is plenty to keep you entertained inland, with many interesting natural attractions, wildlife and cultural points of significance, namely the Bonaire Museum and Washington-Slagbaai National Park.

Washington-Slagbaai National Park

One Bonaire's top attractions, this national park covers almost 20 percent of the land, or 5,643 hectares to be exact. It is a magnificent place to discover the island's wildlife, from turtles to flamingos, and sublime landscapes, which include mangroves, sand dunes and forests. Launched in 1969, the park welcomes around 23,000 visitors every year and has an information desk close to the entrance to teach visitors about the heritage and culture of the island. Address: Malmok, Bonaire Phone: +599-788-9015 Website: http://www.washingtonparkbonaire.org/index.html

Bonaire Museum

Located on the outskirts of the Kralendijk, the Bonaire Museum is set in a charming 130-year old villa. Exhibits include local sculptures, art and pottery that offer insight into the lives and culture of the community. Some of the impressive displays include paintings by local artist Winifred Dania. The museum was the first of its kind and is still the largest on the island. It also focuses on the study of plantation house architecture, which can be seen throughout the island. Address: Kaya J Ree 7 Kralendijk Phone: +599-717-8868.

The Grotto of Lourdes

In 1958, local resident Emma Pourier visited Lourdes, the France-based holy place of worship to commemorate the 100th anniversary since the supposed apparition of the Virgin Mary. Upon her return to Bonaire, she convinced the local priest to create a shrine on the island to spread and enhance the Catholic religion. A suitable cave was found near the town of Rincon and the grotto was constructed. Today, both locals and visitors can enjoy a trip to the shrine for a peaceful moment of reflection in front of the statue. Address: Rincon, Bonaire Phone.

The King's Storehouse

Bonaire's second oldest building, the Mangazina di Rei, or King's Storehouse was initially used to house a large quantity of the island's crops and largest export, salt. These days, the structure is slightly more glamorous, home to a botanical garden, museum and community center. The exhibits explore the anthropological and architectural history of the island and has numerous replicas of traditional stone houses which once formed Bonaire's townscape. Address: Rincon, Bonaire.

Boka Onima

Folklore states that Boka Onima was the arrival point of the first man to Bonaire. A practically impossible destination on which to land due to the surrounding cliffs and sloping beaches, the inlet primarily draws crowds today because of the nearby rock drawings. The age of these primitive works is yet to be determined, but it is believed to be the creation of the Caiqueto Indians whose art has also been found in caves on the South American mainland. Address: East coast, Bonaire

Butterfly Garden
A tropical oasis of nature and tranquility nestled in Bonaire's beautiful flora, the Butterfly Garden exhibits a wide array of species native to the island and surrounding area, primarily Costa Rica. Located on the outskirts of Kralendijk, the farm is easily accessed from the capital and is open from Tuesday to Sunday. The Butterfly Garden is also home to a highly-regarded restaurant which serves up some great dishes while you relax in the shaded garden around a pond brimming with koi fish. Address: Kaminda Lac 101, Kralendijk, Bonaire Website: http://www.butterflygardenbonaire.com/

Donkey Sanctuary
Formed in 1993 to look after the island's wounded and orphaned donkeys, the sanctuary now provides shelter to most of the population of Bonaire's donkeys. The sanctuary is home to more than 400 animals, which is always increasing. Many donkeys are rescued and treated, where they are able to live out their years in

peace and any money raised goes back into the upkeep of the facility. There is also a placid garden where visitors can relax and admire the native iguanas and turtles, or look out over the salt planes to catch a glance of a flamingo.

Shopping and Leisure

While Bonaire is not particularly recognized as a great shopping destination, there are some great outlets with enticing and reasonably priced goods. Unlike many other Caribbean hotspots, the island is not littered with souvenir shops selling trinkets and the usual over-priced vacation gifts. There is one quirky shopping avenue in Kralendijk, featuring a variety of small, boutiques and unique merchants from Dutch cheese to Cuban cigars. Reasonably priced, high-quality china and gold jewelry can also be found on this stretch.

A number of shops within the resorts offer products and prices comparable to those back in the US and Europe. It is worth noting that Cuban cigars cannot be imported back to the US. A trip to the Bonaire arts and crafts market is also highly-recommended if you want to get a flavor of the local scene and purchase gifts to take home.

The original downtown buildings along Kaya Grandi date back to the late 1800's, traditionally housing families upstairs and shops below. Some of these have been renovated and restored, providing an air of authenticity and a charming atmosphere. If you are lucky enough to be in Bonaire on the first Saturday of the month, head over to Rincon Street Market and practice your haggling skills amongst the ramshackle collection of stalls.

There are also a few malls on the island, which cater to the everyday requirements of most travelers and are useful places to pick up clothes, toiletries and food. A number of stores, particularly in the open-air Harborside Mall, focus on equipment for diving, windsurfing and other marine activities, in addition to beachwear. High-end cosmetics and perfumers are also found in abundance, in addition to a wide assortment of liquors and wines. Reductions on duty-free imports make these products fairly cheap, but it is always advised to check how much you can bring back. Bear in mind it is illegal to take sea fans, coral and conch shells off the island.

Free Duty for U.S citizens

Duty Free info for U.S. citizens
U.S. citizens, regardless of age, who have been out of the country for a minimum of 48 hours and who have not used their respective duty-free allowance within 30 days are entitled to a $600 duty-free

tax exemption. Families traveling together can pool their exemptions, meaning couples can bring hone $2,400 worth of articles duty-free.

Liquor: The duty-free allowance for U.S. citizens age 21 and over is one quart, the value of whih must be included within the $600 exemption.

Duty Free info for Canadian citizens
Canadian citizens who have been outside Canada for a minimum of seven days are permitted a duty-free exemption of $750 (Canadian Dollars). Citizens are also permitted a duty-free exemption of $200 (Canadian Dollars) each time they are out of the country for more than 48 hours. Please note that this $200 exemption may not be claimed during the same period as the $750 exemption, nor can your exemptions be pooled with your spouse and/or children.

Liquor: The duty-free allowance for Canadian citizens (who meet the legal age of the province they re-enter) is 40 ounces of wine or liquor or two dozens 12-ounce cans of beer, the value of which must be included within the yearly or quarterly exemption.

Festivals and Events
Bonaire has a rich culture and as a result is home to many festivals throughout the year. One of the island's most celebrated gatherings

is naturally Dive into Adventure, which incorporates numerous marine events. Music is also a pivotal part of the island's identity and every May Bonaire Heineken Jazz Festival comes to town, drawing many international visitors.

Bonaire Carnival

Late February/early March sees the most colorful and spectacular festival of the island's calendar and is one of the best times of the year to visit Bonaire. No matter where you go, it is virtually impossible to escape the party atmosphere and the beat of the Caribbean drum once it's in full-swing. The most elaborate and hedonistic celebrations tend occur on the streets of Kralendijk where everybody puts on crazy costumes and does away with their inhibitions. The dancing, drink and downright debauchery goes on for days with music, fireworks and huge parades.

Simadan Festival

A folk festival held in April, the celebration was originally a harvest event. Originally farmers, with the assistance of friends and family, would head to the fields to rake in the crop. It remains a family-orientated day with lavish feasts thrown, which tend to include signature dishes such as goat soup, giambo (okra soup) and repa (pancakes). The wapa, a traditional dance which involves rows of people moving simultaneously, is a highlight and sees most townsfolk join in.

Bonaire Dive Festival
Bonaire has hosted this dive festival every June since 1997, which focuses primarily on conservation. Non-profit organization CORAL (Coral Reef Alliance) hold the event annually in order to raise awareness of the preservation of marine beauty. The two-week event includes seminars, environmental awareness projects, underwater dives and cocktail parties.

Bonaire Heineken Jazz Festival
Held every July, Bonaire's jazz fest has been running since 2005. The main event takes place on Saturday night, while many other concerts and activities are held across the area. Each year, hundreds of visitors and established musicians head to the island for a number of workshops and interactive events help to promote jazz and music among the young population.

Bonaire International Sailing Regatta
An annual sailing event every October, the Bonaire regatta includes a variety of boat races along the coast. Vessels from around the world come to compete, while numerous windsurfing and freestyle competitions take place. After sunset, attention turns back to the shoreline, notably the Sea Promenade, Wilhelmina Park and

Kralendijk, where jovial, usually booze-fueled, social events go on late into the evening.

Things to Do

Bonaire is a perfect retreat for those looking to relax and soak up the natural wonders found on the island and surrounding coastline. The abundance of marine wildlife and spectacular coral reefs draw visitors from around the globe to the blue depths of the Caribbean. Onshore, flora, fauna and an endless array of birds make for some great walks, treks and bicycle rides and there are a number of tour operators on hand to help you get the most out of your stay on this beautiful island.

Many visitors base themselves in the capital city of Kralendijk, Bonaire's main gateway from where a plethora of diving, snorkeling and boat tours depart. In addition to marine activities, there are an abundance of things to pursue inland, including hiking, horseback riding and cycling through the rugged backdrop and brilliant scenery.

Diving is by far the biggest pull to this charming Caribbean island, and with more than 50 dive sites and unspoiled coral reefs it's obvious why. The calm and unique waters around Bonaire make it ideal for diving throughout the year and with an annual 'nature tag' it is possible to explore the marine park year-round. An endless number of dive operators are located throughout Bonaire, including Captain Don's Habitat and Great Adventures Bonaire.

Bonaire is also renowned for it ideal windsurfing conditions, particularly around Lac Bay. The large, protected bay with its steady winds and year-round sunshine make it one of the world's top destinations for novices and professionals alike. Bonaire Windsurf Place provides lessons and rents equipment.

One of the best ways to uncover the diverse wildlife and natural beauty is on a hiking tour. The dirt roads and goat trails scattered around Bonaire are ideal for scaling, especially in the Washington Slagbaai National Park, which also has the island's highest peak, Brandaris Hill. Tours can be arranged through various operators, such as Rincon-based Soldachi Tours.

Another great way to check out Bonaire's fascinating scenery is horseback riding. The island is home to two stables which offer a few scenic routes along the beach and the backroads, visiting small communities and getting a feel for life as an islander. Rancho-Washikemba, on Bonaire's eastern coast, offers lessons and tours.

If you fancy trying your luck on the tables, gambling while the sun sets overhead is a great way to pass the time. Divi Flamingo Casino is an easy-going venue that has Blackjack, Roulette and slot machines, and is the Caribbean's only barefoot casino open daily.

Bird watching is an extremely popular pastime on the island due to the wide range of species which call the area home. More than 190 different varieties are present, including the Amazon parrot, parakeets and Bonaire's most famous resident, the pink flamingo. A flamingo sanctuary is located on the island, but it is not open to the public. It is possible to catch a glimpse of these timid creatures on tours organized by Bonaire Dive & Adventure.

Museum
Want to see more of Bonaire than fish and coral reefs?

A trip to one of Bonaire's museums is just the ticket to find out more about the local culture and history.

Bonaire Museum The Museo Boneriano (The Museum of Bonaire) the first and largest of Bonaire's museums is located just outside of town on 'Kaya Sabana' and 'Kaya J.C. van der Ree' and is an easy walk from the shopping district. (If you have trouble finding it, just ask where the ice company is and follow the signs from there)

It is housed in a 110 year old building that has been restored to its original splendor. The building itselfs is a study in island plantation house architecture and follows a typical plan used in most of the early houses (one of the exhibits shows the plans used in early construction techniques). The Museum is funded by the Department of Culture and supported by grants, admission fees and donations. A very modest entrance fee of about $2 per person is charged.

Bonaire's other museum is located at the northern end of the island at the entrance of the Washington-Slagbaai National Park. An original plantation house has been restored and serves as a museum. The rooms have been converted into viewing galleries where displays of plantation life, wildlife, geogoly, tools and other articles can be seen free of charge. Donations are accepted. Much of the work done to maintain and construct the displays at the museum is in the capable hands of Mr. George Tholdé. A trip to the museum will certainly reward you with an afternoon well spent. Opposite the museum is another structure which at one time was used as a small store for the plantaion workers to purchase essentials. It now serves as the administration and entrance fee payment window.

Night Life

There are a couple of disco's on Bonaire for those who want to dance the night away. If you want to keep it down but don't want to go to bed yet, then there are a number of bars and cafes to go to on the Oceanside.

There are many more things to do in the Bonaire nightlive.

There is aslo the possibility to go to the casino. There are two casino's, Flamingo Beach and Plaza Resort, available on the island which offers blackjack, poker, slot machines,roulette and other games and close at 2am or 4am. Flamingo is open every day except on the Sunday. Plaza resort is open 7 days a week.

Rock Climbing

Many visitors to Bonaire think it is a bit too quiet, but that really depends on the kind of vacation you want to have. If you are a fan of mass-tourism and want big cities, many shops and a busy nightlife, you will not find it here. But, if you are the outdoor-type and love sun, sea, nature and relaxing by being active, Bonaire has a lot to offer.

For those who can not live without altitude, there is even a possibility to go climbing on Bonaire's beautiful cliffs. Driving along the road to Rincon you will see some nice rock formations that will give a climbing addict sweaty palms. On our sister island of Aruba, the first climbing trails were opened in 1997 and 1998, while on Bonaire the rocks are still untouched. Both Aruba, and Bonaire have the same type of limestone formations. The rocks are the result of the labor of tiny coral polyps over millions of years. You will be climbing on the remains of a reef that has risen above sea level by action of subterranean plates being pushed together.

A real challenge for the pioneets among the climbing fanatics will be to actually open the first climbing trails. Because there are no anchors anywhere to relay on, you will have to bring a complete set of gear including various sizes of nuts and anchors. Bring various sizes because everywhere you look you will find holes in the stone due to erosion. Climbing is a new activity that will eventually spread it's way to Bonaire. If you want your first taste, try Brandaris Hill ins Washington Slagbaai National Park. The only special equipment you will need for that is a good pair of boots or sneakers and a strong constitution.

Brandaris Hill (241 meters/784 feet) is the highest point on Bonaire and offers a panoramic vista of the island. A footpath leads from the parking lot up the ridge. The round-trip walk takes about 2 to 3 hours. The trail is well marked and easy to follow. Once at the top, you can see almost the entire island and also catch a glimpse of Curacao which lies on the western horizon. On especially clear days, even Venezuela is visible.

Be sure to wear good foot protection as a lot of the path is rocky. A water bottle is also a good idea as well as a hat. You should plan to start your climb early (8am) in the day when it is a bit cooler.

Sailing & Boating

Bonaire has along tradition with the sea. Her sailors were known throughout the Caribbean for their skill in navigation and sailing abilities. During the past World Wars, the island men were part of the merchant marine and many gave their lives in the struggle. A monument, placed by Eleanor Roosevelt and dedicated to these 34 brave men, can be found in town opposite Wilhelmina Park.

Bonaire was, and to some extent still is, known as a boat building center. Local craftsman produced some of the finest vessels that were so well built that many are still afloat and in use today. You will see them heading out and returning each afternoon bearing the cath of the day. As a visitor to the island, you should not miss the chance of spending some time sailing our calm water.

Granted, the ships that take you out are more modern, but the feeling of being at sea is the same. There are a number of charters that can take day sailors to snorkel, swim and picnic or just enjoy the beautiful views

Snorkeling Tips

Bonaire is not only one of the world's best diving destinations but also a paradise for snorkelers. Snorkeling is a true family affair, everyone can take part. It's easy to learn, requires a minimum of preparation, and can be enjoyed at anytime of day or night. There are several outfitters that cater to those who want to try the sport. The equipment essentials, mask, fins and snorkel are inexpensive to rent, approximately $10 per day making snorkeling an affordable way to explore the underwater wildlife that is an integral part of the Bonaire experience. Bonaire is unique in offering so many shore accessible snorkeling sites.

Highly recommended are dusk and evening snorkels where one can observe a dramatic changing of the guard, as the reef's fascinating night dwellers make their appearance.

The video below helps illustrate Bonaire's beautiful underwater world from the perspective of a snorkeler.

Here are a few tips to help you enjoy the experience. Be sure to wear sun screen to prevent sun burn. Cover your back and don't forget the back of the legs. For those with not so full a head of hair, a baseball cap is a must. Don't forget, Bonaire is a tropical desert island. At night it is advisable to wear a light dive skin to protect *yourself from the chills and the off chance of some microscopic organisms that might affect tender skin*

Basic snorkeling skills (reviewed in the island wide Introduction to Bonaire Guided Snorkeling) are designed to make sure you are comfortable with your equipment and can float around the reef, completely relaxed and enjoying the underwater world. There are easy skills to master, particularly with the help of a guide. As you get more and more accustomed to snorkeling, you will feel an urge to dive down and take a closer look at the marine life. This is called freediving and consists of holding your breath, making surface dive and slowly exploring the reef. While it's not difficult, most people (particularly beginners) are not immediately comfortable doing it and most of the reasons for this are easy to sole!

The first area to consider is your natural buoyancy. Some people are floaters; other are sinkers. This has to do with the relative size of your lungs (in proportion to total body size), percentage of muscle/fat (muscle weight more than fat) and basic physique. In general, there are far more floaters than sinkers. If you are a floater and try to freedive, you will have to constantly kick to keep yourself underwater. This will quickly deplete your air and energy.

Like everything else in the underwater world, relaxation is the key to freediving. You kick only to move from place to place. How do you offset the natural tendency to float? Your guides will show you how to add a couple of pounds (not much is necessary) of lead weight to a weightbelt, which will offset the natural buoyancy. They'll also help you with your surface dive, which, when you get good, can get you 10 or 15 feet underwater with just one kick. Once you are down, you should be able to hover without kicking, a sure sign you are correctly weighted. See your Bonaire Guide for more help in this very exciting area of advanced snorkelling.

In keeping with the conservation philosophy of the island Bonaire, it is recommended that snorkellers never come in contact with the reef. If you dive down and attempt to stay down by holding on the coral, several things may happen. First of all, you might cut yourself because coral is very, very sharp. Two, the coral might accidentally snap off, destroying several hundred years of growth. Either option is not positive; the guides will be happy to work with you and make you an effortless freediver.

As you get better and better, you will also learn something called the finger touch technique. There are parts of the underwater world safe to touch but you need to know exactly which parts.

These are noncoral areas and you can closely observe corals and marine life by steadying yourself with just the touch of a finger on these parts of the reef. Again, your guides will help you! Snorkel safely (always with a buddy) and responsibly!

How to Select a Snorkel Mask

Fit is the most important criteria in selecting a mask. So how do you buy a mask that fits? It's easy.

Here's How:

✓ Fold the strap over the front of the mask so that it is out of the way.

✓ Hold the mask against your face.

✓ Make sure it fits comfortably around your eyes and nose.

✓ Choose another size if necessary.

✓ While the mask is against your face, inhale through your nose.

✓ The vacuum created in the mask should hold it against your face when you take your hand away.

✓ If the mask doesn't stay put, repeat the process until you find one that does.

Tips:

✓ Don't settle for an ill-fitting mask.

✓ If you find more than one mask that fits, compare the features before making your purchase or rental decision.

How to Clear Your Snorkel

There's no doubt about it. Water will get into your snorkel, whether you submerse yourself intentionaly or a wave splashes water into it. It's an important scuba/snorkel skill you need to know.

Here's How:
✓ Allow yourself to sink below the water until you face is just under the water.

✓ Take a deep breath through your snorkel.

✓ Hold your breath.

✓ Completeley submerse yourself and your snorkel in the water.

✓ Rise to your original position.

✓ Blow a sharp blast of air through your snorkel.

✓ Slowly inhale to see if there is still water in it.

✓ If there is still water in the snorkel, blow another short blast into it.

✓ When the snorkel is clear, continue to breath normally through it.

Tips:

✓ Try not to exhale all your air on the first blast.

✓ When checking to see if the airway is clear don't suck in a huge gulp of air. Do it slowly.

✓ Perfect this skill in a swimming pool first.

Diving and Snorkeling

Bonaire's pristine reefs and diverse marine life are unique to the Caribbean. Because the waters around Bonaire are designated as an official marine park, diving Bonaire is like diving the Caribbean the way it used to be - untouched and unspoiled. The island's location in the south Caribbean gives it an arid climate with little rainfall; consequently, the waters are exceptionally clear of silt, calm, and divable year round. It is an ideal destination for underwater photographers. Water temperatures average a warm 78-84°F (25.6-28.9°C), with visibility often averaging over 100 feet(30m), and frequently, up to 150 feet (55m). During January and February divers may wish to consider a Caribbean dive hood or 3mm shorty to conserve body heat.

Bonaire Marine Park

History:

Bonaire Diving SeahorseIn 1961, while most places were still nailing turtle shells to the wall and slurping turtle soup, Bonaire was enacting legislation to protect sea turtle eggs and nests. In 1971, at a time when divers carried spear guns in much the same way that they today tote underwater cameras, Bonaire banned spearfishing from its reefs. In 1975, the island made it illegal to break coral, take it from the water, or sell it--activities that are still practiced today in the Indo-Pacific. It was no wonder, then, that the government of Bonaire decided to create the Bonaire Marine Park, the next logical step in the island's conservation efforts. With the generous financial support of the World Wildlife Fund of Holland, the Marine Park was established in 1979 . Its purpose is to ensure that Bonaire's marine resources-its magnificent coral reefs, seagrass beds and mangroves-remain intact so that everyone can enjoy our wonderful coral reefs for years to come, just as they are now.

Exploring the Marine Park:

DivingThe Marine Park encompasses approximately 2700 hectares and extends all the way around Bonaire, from the high water mark to the 60m depth contour. Bonaire's narrow, fringing coral reefs encircle both Bonaire and Klein Bonaire. The reefs are very well preserved, very diverse, and support a truly amazing array of reef fish. Recent studies by Dr. Callum Roberts and the volunteer group REEF have shown that Bonaire's fish population is the most diverse in the Caribbean and ranks among the best in the world.

Typically, the reefs start right at the water's edge and shelve off gently to a depth of about 32 feet (10m). This area, known as the reef terrace, is very narrow along the north coast (as little as 20m wide) and much wider in the south, where it may reach widths of 200m. In very shallow waters are encrusting coral formations, which grow close the bottom to avoid wave action. On the reef terrace, you will find amazing stands of elkhorn and staghorn coral, often with fire coral, patch reefs, and dense stands of soft corals--all inhabited by a dazzling spectrum of reef fish. The tangs and parrot fish will be out in force, grazing and keeping the algae stands under control. Expect to see lots of damsel fish, with butterfly and angel fish amid grunts, coneys, rock hinds and their relatives--goatfish, hogfish, and an abundance of wrasse. On the bottom, look for peacock flounder, lizard fish, and scorpionfish, all of which are so well camouflaged that you may easily overlook them. Goatfish, by comparison, are hard to miss. They make no attempt to hide their presence as they churn up the bottom in search of tasty morsels. Be sure to notice the sticky tentacled anemones hiding within the coral.

Then comes a transition to a zone dominated by the mountainous star coral, which may form huge pagoda-like structures, pillars, mounds, or even sloping, overlapping, shingle-like structures. This zone is known as the drop-off zone, and it starts almost uniformly between 10-12m. There may be an abundance of soft corals and Bonaire Reefbeautifully colored sponges, as well as Byzantine stands of mountainous star coral interspersed with clouds of radiant fish. Don't miss the fierce sergeant major fish (they are actually harmless and approximately 8 inches in length) defending their eggs, and moray eels hiding out in crevices. Solitary grouper, large parrotfish, and various snapper can be seen swimming the reef; you can also expect to see the ubiquitous shoaling chromis, bothersome yellowtail snapper, and passing schools of various jacks cruising by in blue water. Specials include tarpon, turtle, seahorses and frogfish. Extra-specials are nurse shark, whale shark, rays and dolphin.

Bonaire CoralBelow the drop-off, the reefs descend sharply, and the mountainous star coral communities described above yield to leaf or scroll corals, which cover the sloping bottom like a beard. This area, known as the reef slope, is also where you will find fine stands of black coral. Beware, the reefs on Bonaire slope down and down and down. The fish here are similar to, but less abundant than, those in the drop-off zone.

Bonaire also has some special reef features, including two examples of spur and groove formations, where the corals form fingers which protrude perpendicular to the shore. Typically, coral formations follow the contours of the coast. Diving BonaireBonaire's reef forms also include buttress formations, where corals have grown out to sea, forming a kind of headland with sandy valleys in between; a very well developed double reef in the south; and several small wall dives. Bonaire also has several large and small wrecks-the most famous is the Hilma Hooker, a freighter which lies on its side at a depth of 30m.

Park Management:
The park is managed by STINAPA, a non-governmental, not for profit organization run by a board of dedicated local professionals who donate their time to protect and conserve the island's natural flora and fauna. In addition to the Marine Park, STINAPA also manages Washington Slagbaai National Park, the Barcadera cave system, RAMSAR sites and Klein Bonaire. The park's staff of twenty-six has a BIG agenda. More than and 60,000 visitors annually keep the personnel very busy.

Park Rules:

✓ Please make sure that you follow our park rules and report any infringements you may see.

✓ No anchoring. Anchoring is prohibited everywhere!

✓ Public moorings may be used by any vessel up to 38' on first come, first serve basis for up to two hours. You MUST put out a scope line which is as long as your vessel.

✓ Spear fishing is completely prohibited.

✓ Do not take anything out of the water (except garbage).

✓ Divers and snorkelers should make as little contact with the reefs as possible: don't sit, stand or hold on to coral.

✓ Divers should make sure they are neutrally buoyant and stow gloves.

✓ Do not take any corals, sea fans, shells or the like out of Bonaire.

✓ Turtles are completely and internationally protected. Do not be tempted to buy shells or other turtle by-products or you will be fined heavily!

✓ Conch are also internationally protected. Taking back one shell may cost you dearly.

✓ Contact the Bonaire Marine Park to report any infringements at tel: 717 84444

Usage Fees
STINAPA has instituted usage fees designated to help preserve and protect the Bonaire National Marine Park. Divers are charged a US$25 fee, good for a year while windsurfers and kiteboarders pay a US$10 fee. These tags are usually available at the island's outfitters, activity operators and most hotels. The dive tags and receipt also allow free access to Washington Slagbaai National Park--always worth a visit.

Mooring Fees
Since November 1, 1999, yachts arriving on Bonaire do not have to play "musical moorings" when they make landfall. On that date, the Harbour Village Marina began managing the 40 visiting yacht moorings owned by the Bonaire Marine Park. Moorings are assigned by the Marina and can be arranged in advance by VHF. Arriving vessels proceed to the arrival dock at the Marina, clear the port authority, customs and immigration there, be given information on the Marine Park regulations, then proceed to their designated mooring.

Harbour Village Marina manages the moorings in the bay off Kralendijk. These are available, at $10 per night, to visiting yachts no more than 18 meters.

Under its contract with STINAPA, Harbour Village Marina will also be responsible for maintaining the moorings. New mooring lines have been installed, and the Marina says it intends to replace the PVC spars with something more suitable. As in the past, no liability for loss or damage will be assumed by STINAPA or the Marina. Captains will be responsible for checking the mooring lines to make sure their boat is secure. They are also responsible for leaving the mooring during adverse weather conditions, such as the heavy wave action caused by the recent westerly.

Private and Commercial Moorings
Private or commercial moorings require a permit. The cost is $ 280 per year per mooring. Moorings may be used to tie off boats, floats, swim platforms or for swim lines etc.

Fishing boats, registered with the Harbormaster, 12 feet or shorter, with a maximum 25 hp engine, are exempt from the yearly fee.

Finally, please be sure to take all your garbage home with you from your outings. Our motto is "tene Boneiru limpi" (Keep Bonaire clean).

Scuba Diving

Looking for Scuba Paradise? You need to look no further. Bonaire is known to the insiders as being in the top three scuba dive destinations in the world. Beautiful underwater landscapes, crystal clear waters, and a large score of professional and experienced diving operators. The underwater crown jewels are well protected by the Bonaire Marine Park, who have enforce the "Look but don't touch"-rule since its inception in 1979.

Bonaire has always been a pioneer when it comes to protecting its marine environment. In 1961 Bonaire enforced legislation to protect its turtle poputation. Ever since 1971 it is forbidden to use spear guns and in 1975 it was made illegal to brake off live coral.

Bonaire Dive Orientation

If you are planning a trip to Bonaire and have a scuba dive/hotel package you will be given a thorough dive orientation and briefing before your first dive on the island. One of the Bonaire Marine Park Regulations is for all visitors to do a check-out dive as part of the briefing process before taking off on their own to shore dive or going on a dive boat. The main reasons for this are to have each scuba diver check buoyancy so that damage to the reef is minimized or eliminated and also to check out their dive equipment, whether it be rented or owned.

Also, every scuba diver on Bonaire must purchase a Marine Park Tag (US$25) valid for one calendar year. Orientation procedures vary from dive center to dive center, so it's a good idea to check in early.

How to Select a Scuba Snorkel Mask

Fit is the most important criteria in selecting a scuba mask. So how do you buy a mask that fits? It's easy.

Here's How:

- ✓ Fold the strap over the front of the mask so that it is out of the way.

- ✓ Hold the mask against your face.

- ✓ Make sure it fits comfortably around your eyes and nose.

- ✓ Choose another size if necessary.

- ✓ While the mask is against your face, inhale through your nose.

- ✓ The vacuum created in the mask should hold it against your face when you take your hand away.

- ✓ If the mask doesn't stay put, repeat the process until you find one that does.

Tips:

✓ Don't settle for an ill-fitting mask.

✓ If you find more than one mask that fits, compare the features before making your purchase or rental decision.

How to Clear Your Snorkel

There's no doubt about it. Water will get into your snorkel, whether you submerse yourself intentionaly or a wave splashes water into it. It's an important scuba/snorkel skill you need to know.

Here's How:

✓ Allow yourself to sink below the water until you face is just under the water.

✓ Take a deep breath through your snorkel.

✓ Hold your breath.

✓ Completeley submerse yourself and your snorkel in the water.

✓ Rise to your original position.

✓ Blow a sharp blast of air through your snorkel.

✓ Slowly inhale to see if there is still water in it.

✓ If there is still water in the snorkel, blow another short blast into it.

✓ When the snorkel is clear, continue to breath normally through it.

Tips:
✓ Try not to exhale all your air on the first blast.

✓ When checking to see if the airway is clear don't suck in a huge gulp of air. Do it slowly.

✓ Perfect this skill in a swimming pool first.

BonaireBird Watching

Bonaire has no native species of birds, however, there are a number of subspecies, or geographical races that are found on the islands Aruba, Bonaire and Curacao. Bonaire's most famous is the pink flamingo, which most evenings around sunset, you may be able to see small flocks leaving the southern tip of Bonaire, near the Willemstoren Lighthouse. Contrary to popular belief, they are not all flying off to Venezuela, although some undoubtedly will reach the South American coast. There are a number of environmental factors that have made Bonaire a very intresting site for birders to enjoy, and there is always the chance that an alert birder will record the occurrence of an extra-limital bird. The Island boats over 190 species including the Lora, which is now protected against capture by international treaty. There are a number of publications for use by the visiting birder (hopefully obtained beforehand because they cannot be purchased in the islands).

Flora & Fauna

It has become a tradition for many generations to understand the importance of nature and the unique position Bonaire has to conserve it. With this said, Bonaire developed a master plan to control the development of the island without harming its natural wonders.

The old salt pans of Pekelmeer, posed an ecological problem: Bonaire has one of the largest Caribbean flamingo colonies in the Western Hemisphere, and these birds build their conical mud nests in the salt pans. Pleas from wildlife conservationists convinced the company that it should set aside an area of 56 ha for a flamingo sanctuary, with access strictly prohibited. The birds, initially rather startled by the sudden activity, have settled into a peaceful co-existence, so peaceful in fact that they have actually doubled their output and are now laying two eggs a year instead of their previous one.

There are said to be over 15,000 flamingoes on the island, and they can be seen wading in Goto Meer Bay in the northwest, in the salt lake near Playa Grandi, and in Lac Bay on the southeast coast of

Bonaire, feeding on algae which give them their striking rose-pink colour. It is an impressive sight to witness the flamingoes rising from the water in the evening as they prepare to overnight in Venezuela.

There are also two smaller bird sanctuaries at the Salt Pans and Goto Meer. At Posi Mangel, in the national park, thousands of birds gather in the late afternoon. Bronswinkel Well, also in the park, is another good place to see hundreds of birds and giant cacti. The indigenous Bonaire Green Parrot can be seen in the Park and at Onima. About 190 species of birds have been found on Bonaire as well as the flamingoes. An annual Birdwatching Olympics and Nature Week is held in September, with prizes for those who spot the greatest number of species.

There are lots of iguanas and lizards of all shapes and sizes. The big blue lizards are endemic to Bonaire, while the Anolis, a tree lizard with a yellow dewlap, is related to the Windward Islands Anolis species rather than to the neighbouring Venezuelan species. The interior has scant vegetation but the enormous cacti provide perching places for yellow-winged parrots. The most common mammal you are likely to see is the goat, herds of which roam the island eating everything in sight except the cacti.

Flamingos

The Flamingo, protected on Bonaire, is the island's signature bird. Bonaire is one of the only Flamingo breeding sites in the Southern Caribbean. The Flamingo Reserve, nestled among the salt pans on Bonaire's southern tip, is a special breeding ground for the birds. Admittance is prohibited to the reserve as flamingos are very sensitive to disturbances, but often time flamingos can be seen from the road. Additionally, flamingos may be spotted at Goto Lake, Slagbaai, Playa Funchi and other saltpans.

Over 210 species of birds can be seen on the island, many of them clustered around Goto Lake, Pekelmeer, Cai and Dos Pos. Spotting each species depends to some extent on migration patterns and the weather (in the dry season, for example, normally shy birds approach towns in search of water). Bonaire's birds can be classified into three categories: sea birds, shore birds, and land birds. The flamingo, Bonaire's national symbol, is technically a shore bird, but its beauty, rarity, and unique presence on the island places the bird in a class by itself.

There are only four places in the world where Flamingo on Bonairelarge numbers of Caribbean Flamingos breed -- Bonaire is one of them. You can see allusions in the walls of the pink-painted airport, in the endless flamingo T-shirts, and in the array of flamingo kitch for sale on the streets of Kralendjik, but the birds themselves appear to be entirely absent, carefully hidden on some Bonairean backstage.

This wariness seems to be unnatural: if nature ever dressed a diva, the flamingo is it. The pink cotton candy feathers, the graceful, wavy neck, and the long sinewy legs all seems to cry "look at beautiful me," but in reality flamingos prefer anything but a spotlight. In fact, the birds are so sensitive to noise and intrusion that the slightest disturbance will cause them to quickly flee. They will never come close to people.

There are two places to see Bonaire's flamingos. One is at the Pekelmeer Sanctuary to the south, where the birds flock around the salt ponds; the other at FlamingosLake Gotomeer, in Washington Slagbaai National Park in the north. At both places, it is important to keep your distance and not disturb the birds. Bonaireans are as protective of their flamingos as they are of their reefs. The best way to get a great photograph is to bring a telephoto lens. On a good day, you can see them gather by the hundreds in a chaotic, undulating pink cloud. The pinkness of their feathers actually comes from the carotene found in their diet of brine shrimp, brine fly pupae, small clams, and other micro-delectables.

Flamingos are social animals, and a minimum of 15 to 20 animals is required before they'll begin to breed. They mate for life, and what actually causes them to nest and breed is still something of a mystery (though several studies suggest that a good rainfall is highly influential). Once a pair does mate, both the male and the female share equally in the tasks of building a nest, sitting on their single egg for about a month, and feeding the chick. After about three months, the chick will be able make the 90 kilometer flight to Venezuela, a trip the flamingos make when food on Bonaire becomes scarce.

Birds
Sea Birds
Sea BirdsThe magnificent frigatebird (Fregata magnificens) is the most common sea bird spotted off shore. It is notable for its wing span, the largest in relation to body weight of any bird. It is also known as the man o' war bird, and the comparison to warships is a particularly apt one--with its superior size and flight capabilities, the frigate bird harasses less agile flyers like pelicans, egrets, and cormorants until they drop their catch. The male frigate is notable in having an all black head and body. They do not breed on Bonaire so males with a red throat sac, are seldom seen.

One of the birds it often steals from is the brown booby (Sulal eucogaster). These large sea birds are mainly brown, with white breasts and bellies. They have long, pointed wings and a torpedo-shaped body and can often be seen perched off shore or flying over water. They are excellent divers and can also swim underwater in pursuit of fish.

PelicanOther sea birds are the olivaceous cormorant (Phalacrocorax olivaceus) and the brown pelican (Pelecanus occidentalis), both of which can be spotted perched on piers or rocks near the water. The cormorant has a black body, a long, thin neck, and a slender, yellowish bill slightly hooked at the tip. It swims with its body low in the water, diving for food. The pelican is brown-grey, with yellowish-white on the head. Magnificent divers, they often swoop down from impressive heights, plunging into the water like cannonballs.

Shore Birds
Bonaire is home to five different species of herons, and they are among the most common wading birds on the island. The largest is the great blue heron (Ardea herodias), which reaches heights of 125 cm (50 inches). It is usually found near water in mangroves, ponds, salt pans, or on rocks off the seashore. They have blue-grey backs and white heads, with a black plume running from the beak over

the eye. The other herons of the island are the black-crowned night heron (Nycticorax nycticorax), the yellow-crowned night heron (Nyctanassa violacea), the tricolored heron (Egretta tricolor) and the striated heron (Butorides striatus).

Egrets are another common wading bird. The snowy egret (Egretta thula) usually congregates in groups of four or five, feeding in ponds or perched near water. It is all white, except for its black bill and legs and bright yellow feet (it is nicknamed "Golden Slippers"). The reddish egret (Egretta rufescens) has two color phases: a white phase and a dark phase (with slate-grey feathers and cinnamon-brown head and neck). It's worth trying to catch a glimpse of reddish egrets feeding: they stagger through the shallows with their wings outstretched, balancing precariously while they stab the water, anxiously on the hunt. The great white egret (Egretta alba) is often seen with other waders near mangroves or hunched on branches over water. It is entirely white, except for a yellow bill and black legs.

Many of Bonaire's smaller shore birds are called "peeps," a general term for all those species which are impossible to identify in winter or non-breeding plumage. Peeps are small (about 13-18 cm or 5-6 inches), and include such species as the semi-palmated plover

(Charadrius semipalmatus), the snowy plover (Charadrius alexandrinus) and the semi-palmated sandpiper (Calidris pusilla).

Other birds commonly seen on the shore include the short-billed dowitcher (Limnodromus griseus), which probes in mud or shallow water with its straight, long bill, and the whimbrel (Numenius phaeopus), distinguished by its very long, curved bill. Gulls and terns can also be seen circling above the coasts or perched on rocks. The laughing gull (Larus atricilla), so called for its distinctive loud cry, is a year-round resident on Bonaire. The least tern (Sterna albifrons) is abundant in the spring and summer, while the royal tern (Sterna maxima) is seen year-round. The common tern (Sterna birundo) is seen only in the summer.

Land Birds
Yellow Shouldered ParrotTwo tropical birds found only on Bonaire are the Caribbean parakeet (Aratinga pertinax, subspecies xanthogenius) and the yellow-shouldered parrot (Amazona barbadensis, subspecies rothschildi). While both birds have bright green plumage, it's easy to tell them apart by the color of the head: the parakeet has a yellowish-orange face, while that of the parrot is yellow (and a smaller proportion of the face is colored). Parakeets are also more numerous; they can be seen anywhere on the island where there is vegetation. The best places to see parrots are in the

cactus fields of the north and in fruit-bearing trees (especially mangoes). The parrot is endangered with an island population of only 700-800. Bonaire is a critical breeding ground for the survival of this species.

Only skilled and patient birdwatchers will catch glimpses of the island's notoriously shy pigeons. The red-necked pigeon (Columba squamosa), so named for its purple-red head and neck, usually hides in rock crevices or high in trees. The bare-eyed pigeon (Columba corensis), one of the largest on the island, can sometimes be spotted in trees or scrub foliage. It is silvery-grey, with a bare patch of bluish skin around the eye. Notable is the white stripe on the wing.

Bonaire is also home to several birds of prey, the most common of which is the osprey (Pandion haliaetus). Mostly dark, it has a white head and is easily distinguished by the prominent dark stripe which runs across the head through the eye. Osprey scan the water from above, then suddenly drop to the surface and snatch their prey with their formidable talons. The crested caracara (Polyborus plancus), which looks like a hawk with a vulture's beak, is frequently seen atop cacti, or eating carrion.

Bonaire HummingbirdBonaire's two species of hummingbirds appear erratically. The ruby-topaz hummingbird (Chrysolampis mosquitus) is the larger species. The male has an iridescent, brilliant red crown and an orange-gold throat, while the female has a dark bronze-green back. The male common emerald hummingbird (Chlorostilbon mellisugus) is such a deep green that it can sometimes appear black. The female has a green back and head, with a white stripe over the eye.

The tropical mockingbird (Mimus gilvus) sings incessantly, often mimicking other birds. It is ubiquitous, happy anywhere where there's a hint of shade. The bananaquit (Coereba flaveola), Bonaire's most common bird, can be seen everywhere on the island.

Below is a small sampling of land birds that belong to the warbler family and are represented by as many as 34 very colorful species seen in the vivid breeding plumage of the spring male. They come through Bonaire on their migration to their nesting grounds in the United States, and Canada.

Stinapa

Stichting Nationale Parken (STINAPA), manages the protected Bonaire National Marine and Washington Slagbaai National Parks.

Founded in 1962 as STINAPA Netherlands Antilles, the objective was to have a foundation actively protecting nature in the Netherlands Antilles. The first activities were concentrated on Bonaire. Efforts were made to safeguard the breeding grounds of the Caribbean flamingo and then to create the Washington Park in 1969 - the first sanctuary of the Netherlands Antilles. In 1979, funds were raised and Slagbaai plantation completed the park.

STINAPA manages the protected areas of Bonaire, communicates with Park visitors and cares for the preservation and conservation of nature on Bonaire in general.

STINAPA is dedicated to the conservation of Bonaire's natural and historical heritage through the sustainable use of its resources. See video >>

A few Flamingo facts: Caribbean flamingos have the brightest coloration and are pink because of a diet rich in alpha and beta carotenoid pigments found in algae and insects. Flamingos mainly lay one egg, and chicks are grey and white. In order to fly, flamingos have to get a running start! Did you know that flamingos have little or no sense of smell?

Karko Project

STINAPA launched a Queen Conch Restoration Project in Lac in 2010. Lac is the largest bay in the Dutch Caribbean and is not only a critical habitat for Bonaire and the region, but also a RAMSAR site, recognized globally as wetlands of special significance. Lac is a nursery for reef fish and a feeding area for green sea turtle. Also it is an important resting and nesting place for numerous birds and marine invertebrates, including the Queen Conch or Karko. Earlier this shellfish was found in large quantities, but due to overfishing, the population has diminished drastically. Therefore STINAPA started an outreach campaign focusing on the Queen Conch which engages every sector of the local community from schools and daycare centers to churches and the business sector. The slogan of the project was as follows: "Ban trese karko bek, Laga nan na pas pa mañan nos tin mas!" roughly translates to "Bring our conch back; Leave them alone so we can have more tomorrow!"

Coral Restoration Project

Diving in unspoiled nature? Bonaire is known in the world for the way it protects its nature. That's why in 2012 the Bonaire island council granted a permit to the Coral Restoration Foundation (CRF) to begin developing a coral nursery and reef restoration project in Bonaire.

The goal of the foundation is to restore degraded portion of the reef, in particular the shallow water population of staghorn and elkhorn corals around Bonaire and the adjacent island Klein Bonaire.

The main production nursery is situated on Klein Bonaire, where the coral is disturbed as little as possible and more nurseries are located in front of Buddy Dive Resort and Harbour Village which are used for training and demonstrations. The total nursery coral capacity is almost 7000 corals.

CRF works together with local businesses and dive operators, like Buddy Dive Resort and Great Adventures Bonaire to keep restoring the reef, promote awareness and involve and train tourists and local people as Coral Restoration divers

Sea Turtle Conservation Bonaire

Sea Turtle Conservation Bonaire (STCB) is a non-governmental research and conservation organization that has been protecting sea turtles since 1991. The small Caribbean island of Bonaire is home to three of the world's six endangered or critically endangered species of marine turtles: the hawksbill, green, and loggerhead turtle. Green and hawksbill turtles can be seen year-round, while loggerheads generally visit only during the nesting season.

STCB mission is to ensure that Bonaire's sea turtles have a secure future, and to connect people to sea turtle conservation in ways that inspire caring for nature.

The organization uses best practices in science and conservation to build knowledge and protection of Bonaire's sea turtles. STCB shares their knowledge to raise awareness, affect policy and build support for biodiversity protection.

Echo Bonaire

Echo is a non-governmental conservation organization that has been protecting the Yellow-shouldered Amazon Parrots (loras) on Bonaire since 2010. The small Caribbean island of Bonaire is one of only a few locations in the world where these parrots can be found. Globally, the population is estimated to be between 2500-7500 and on Bonaire there are about 1000 parrots. Because of their limited range and small numbers, these parrots are listed as Vulnerable to the threat of extinction.Echo's mission is to safeguard the future of the Yellow-shouldered Amazon Parrot on Bonaire. It pursues this through conservation, education and outreach using research as a tool to inform these efforts.

Echo's current conservation work is focused on the following actions:

- ✓ Reducing the poaching of chicks for the local and international pet trade.

- ✓ Restoring the dry-forest habitat that the parrots call home.

- ✓ Reducing habitat degradation by non-native species such as donkeys, goats, and pigs

Sustainability

So many buzzwords seem to be circulating these days when it comes to the environment, sustainable, carbon neutral, carbon footprint, balanced, offset, greenhouse emissions, eco-tourism.

So how do we fit them into the scheme of things?

Bonaire is striving to become Carbon Neutral. Our goal is to become a tourism destination that is in balance. We will have our gas emissions (GHG) identified, measured, reduced where possible and 100 percent of the remaining emissions will be offset through high quality renewable energy, energy efficiency and or reforestation projects. This is the easiest way to describe how Bonaire will become a leading carbon neutral destination in the world

Ramsar Sites

The Ramsar Convention is an international treaty that protects wetlands of great international importance with emphasis on the significance of waterfowl. All Ramsar sites registered by the Dutch Caribbean lie within Bonaire: Lac, Pekelmeer, Klein Bonaire, Gotomeer and Slagbaai Lagoon.

Bordered by globally endangered mangroves, numerous waterfowl breed and feed in the area of Lac. The Flamingo Sanctuary at Pekelmeer is one of the most important breeding grounds for the Southern Caribbean Flamingo population. Klein Bonaire, encircled by a great coral reef, offers flamingo feeding and turtle nesting areas. Gotomeer, foraging site for hundreds of flamingos, contains the most important food source for flamingos: brine fly and larvae. Slagbaai lagoon is a foraging and breeding site for flamingos and other birds like pelicans and herons.

Beaches

Playa Chikitu: Lying in Washington National Park, Playa Chikutu is beautiful, but, alas, swimming is forbidden due to the enormous waves and the dangers that lurk underwater. You would be swept off your feet right after you walked in due to a strong current that passes the island on the north coast

Boka Kokolishi: Also situated on the North Coast, Boka Kokolishi is not suited for swimming, but it is a beautiful place to hike along the rugged shoreline with its typical round shaped pools made of lava stone.

Boka Bartol: This shore dive is the northernmost site in the Marine Park. Advanced divers may encounter strong currents. The recommended depth is from 20-80 feet, with interesting coral formations in the shallows. Many of the larger fish species abound, and there is a chance to see rays and Garden Eels in the sandy bottom.

Playa Funch: i Lying on the Westernmost tip of the island, Playa Fuchi is definitely worth visiting when you want to see iguana's and lizards that roam around freely. It's also one of the recommended sites for a Bonaire Guide Snorkel.

Boka Slagbaai: A beautiful beach, rocky with little sand where you can find spots to lay down your towel. There are buildings dating back to 1869.

Playa Frans: At the North Point near Slagbaai. Hard to reach but definitely worth the effort. A very intimate place, with a quiet surf. You will love it there. But don't tell anyone, it's not a big place...

1000 Steps Beach: Why is it called Thousand Steps? Because it is a long way down from the road. No problem for the young and well-trained, but when you are taking your scuba gear it requires quite an effort. The reward is that there are not many people even though is it a beautiful spot.

Bachelor Beach: Just a few hundres yards south of Playa Mangel is a staircase that leads to a thin strip of sand and a really great place fo a swim. Although there are no real tides on Bonaire, when the water is high it is difficult to lay out so check the waves before spreading your beach towel.

Pink Beach: A great place to snorkel, picnic or scuba dive. Reachable by car, taxi or bike. The flamingo pink bus stops here every day, based on a schedule posted in hotels and dive stores and from 8:30 a.m. to 5 p.m. will provide a variety of services.

Lac Bay: Tranquil waters, a swimming paradise for every one. Every weekend there is bands playing from two in the afternoon, drawing locals and tourists alike.

Getting Around
Car Rentals
Bonaire is fortunate to have a wide choice of well known, reliable car rental agencies.

Even though we are relatively small in size, a car will help you to maximize your

vacation. Since we are known as the shore diving capital of the Caribbean, the most

popular rental vehicle is the double cabin pick-up truck. You are well advised to secure a reservation in advance, especially around holiday periods. Most agencies do have a minimum age requirement of 23-25 years. You will need to have a credit card and a valid driving license. Almost all of the cars are standard shift, so if an automatic is needed, please make your reservations early. Visitors will find the rental vehicles to be late models and in top shape. If you intend to tour the national park, be advised that a jeep type vehicle or pick-up with a high ground clearance is required.

Motorcycle, Scooter and Bicycle Rentals

Not everyone who visits the island rents a car. The best thing next to walking is to rent a scooter or one of the quads. A number of shops now offer the chance to feel the breeze blow through your hair while on board one of these "open air" vehicles. The same rules that apply for car rentals also apply to these motorized forms of transport. For the real freedom lovers, Harley Davidson's are lined up awaiting new riders! Remember, a license and credit card will need to be shown. For the real adventurers, a number of bike rental shops are on hand to rent everything from sedate touring bikes to rugged mountain models that are sure to challenge anyone interested in navigating the miles of marked bike trails. If you are interested in renting one of the alternative vehicles, check out the web sites and make a reservation well in advance.

Transportation & Taxi

Renting a vehicle on Bonaire is the popular means of island transportation. There are

various rental agencies on the island. Transportation providers offer cars, trucks, jeeps,

motorcycles, bicycles, scooters and other "specialty" vehicles. Driving is on the right side of the road and follows international road signs. Drivers are urged to use caution when driving and obey speed limits. The speed limit is 60 kilometers per hour outside urban areas and 40 kilometers per hour inside urban areas. Be cautious of Bonaire's animals, such as donkeys and goats, on the roadway. Cars share the road with pedestrians and cyclists. You can always reach a taxi by calling: +599 717 8100

Cycling

Touring

Because of Bonaire's unique topography, cycling around the island is both interesting and invigorating. At first glance, the predominantly flat terrain lulls you into thinking there is no challenge, but the hilly northern region will tax even the strongest legs.

Miles of paved roads, all suitable for comfortable cycling, meander along the island's sparsely populated coast. To the south are Bonaire's stunning solar salt pans and salt mountains, historic slave huts, and Willemstoren Lighthouse. On the north road cyclists can find majestic ospreys, secluded coves perfect for snorkeling and picnicking, the ancient limestone bench marking the sea's level over 100,000 years ago, and historic Karpata, a restored plantation house

Bonaire's arid, semi-desert interior, with its unpaved roads, lends itself to adventuresome mountain bike touring. Off the beaten path are ranches and agricultural areas, unique bird subspecies like the endemic yellow-shouldered parrot and flamboyant pink flamingoes, fascinating geological formations, and mysterious Caiquetio petroglyphs. Goats, wild donkeys, and the camouflaged iguana live among the prickly cacti and aloe along the way to Rincon, an historic inland village.

Tips

Here are some tips to you may wish to consider before venturing out:

Properly evaluate your skill and fitness levels before beginning your tour

Set goals, plan the route and rest stops

Bring sunblock, comfortable clothing, and a hat or helmet should be considered

Carry plenty of water when travelling alone

Cycling Events

Every November, there is an annual international triathlon, consisting of a 1 km swim course in the open ocean, a 40 km flat terrain road course or 25 km hilly off-road course for bicycles, and a 10 km run through downtown Kralendijk. Information on the race can be obtained from Richard Pietersz at tel: 599-7-8580; fax: 599-7-6550.

Cycle Bonaire

Location Kaya Gob N. Debrot adjacent to the Sand Dollar Resort. Cycle Bonaire shares space with Bonaire Dive and Adventure. They offer daily or weekly rentals of 21-speed TREK mountain bikes, which includes water bottles, a helmet, repair, first aid kits and a lock. Bikes are also available for sale. The staff can provide assistance with choosing a correctly sized bike, learning the local rules of the road and basic off-road skills, and helpful tips and advice about safety. Special guided half-day or full-day excursions, orientation to bike trails and general routes are available as well as trail maps and descriptions. There are even resident bike doctors to make repairs. For additional information, call Andre Nahr at 717 2229.

Clyde Hill